Listening and Reading for English Language Learners

ALSO BY DORIT SASSON

Speaking and Writing for English Language Learners: Collaborative Teaching for Greater Success with K–6

Listening and Reading for English Language Learners

Collaborative Teaching for Greater Success with K–6

Dorit Sasson

ROWMAN & LITTLEFIELD EDUCATION

A division of
ROWMAN & LITTLEFIELD PUBLISHERS, INC.
Lanham • Boulder • New York • Toronto • Plymouth, UK

Published by Rowman & Littlefield Education
A division of Rowman & Littlefield Publishers, Inc.
A wholly owned subsidiary of The Rowman & Littlefield Publishing Group, Inc.
4501 Forbes Boulevard, Suite 200, Lanham, Maryland 20706
www.rowman.com

10 Thornbury Road, Plymouth PL6 7PP, United Kingdom

Copyright © 2014 by Dorit Sasson

All rights reserved. No part of this book may be reproduced in any form or by any electronic or mechanical means, including information storage and retrieval systems, without written permission from the publisher, except by a reviewer who may quote passages in a review.

British Library Cataloguing in Publication Information Available

Library of Congress Cataloging-in-Publication Data

Sasson, Dorit, 1970–
  Listening and reading for English language learners : collaborative teaching for greater success with K–6 / Dorit Sasson.
    pages cm
  Includes bibliographical references and index.

ISBN 978-1-4758-0589-5

 1. English language—Study and teaching (Elementary)—Foreign speakers.
 2. Language arts—Correlation with content subjects.
  I. Title.
PE1128.A2S314 2014
372.652'1—dc23

2013033343

To Haim Sasson for his steadfast and loving support and encouragement and for helping me see this book through.

Contents

Foreword	ix
Preface	xiii
Acknowledgments	xvii
Introduction	xix

1. Introduction to Collaboration for K–6 English Language Learners — 1

   Collaboration past and present, types of collaborative models and configurations, benefits of co-teaching and collaboration, best practices for collaboration, challenges and obstacles, the academic stakes behind collaboration.

2. Collaboration in the Development of Listening Skills — 23

   Common problems, improving reading fluency and comprehension, the role of listening instruction in vocabulary development, strategies on scaffolding academic language and content, second-language-acquisition issues, language objectives, co-teaching situations and models.

3. Collaboration in the Development of Reading Skills — 41

   Distinction of the roles between English proficiency and English language proficiency, critical areas of co-teaching in early primary grades, targeted reading skills and standards, vocabulary and SLA influences, strategies for building background knowledge and other schemata, co-teaching situations and models.

4 Collaboration in the Development of Read-alouds, Academic Vocabulary, and Differentiated Instruction 59

Strategies and techniques for collaborating in the areas of content literacy as it relates to a read-aloud curriculum as well as techniques that support K–6 ELL students learning how to read, applying differentiation techniques, explicit academic teaching of vocabulary to co-teaching, co-teaching situations and models.

Appendix 91

Index 101

Foreword

> The process of English language learners acquiring English literacy is not a mere process of learning the linguistic codes. Rather, the process is dynamic, cultural, and social, and it involves not just the learner but, equally important, the teacher, the text, and the context.
>
> —S. Xu, 2003

> The learner, the teacher, the text, and the context: Sociocultural approaches to early literacy instruction for English language learners.
>
> —D. Barone and L. M. Morrow, 2003

The need to support ELL students within schools to insure their success is of critical importance to U.S. educators. There are certainly many configurations to support ELLs within schools such as bilingual education classes or English language learning support outside of the classroom. However, most mainstream classroom teachers have the primary responsibility for developing students' competence in English and literacy (Au, 2002; Neufeld & Fitzgerald, 2001). Surprisingly many teachers have had little or no professional development focused on facilitating ELLs' English learning and literacy development (Hadaway, Vardell, & Young, 2004). For this reason and others, many teachers find meeting their ELLs' learning needs a challenge. They worry about how to teach a student who does not speak the language of the school.

The centrality of language to learning is an issue that teachers of ELLs wrestle with as they provide instruction. A common situation for many ELLs is, upon entry into school, typically preschool or kindergarten, they are expected to only communicate through a new language, English. These students are often expected to achieve the same literacy competencies as their peers who come to school with a home language of English. Very few of these students ever have extra time in school to learn about reading and writing in English as they learn English and how to read and write. They are typically allotted the same amount of time as students who come to school familiar with English to meet grade-level expectations. This is an enormous challenge for students, teachers, and parents (Nieto, 1999).

Dorit Sasson's book is written directly to teachers in mainstream classes who instruct students whose home language is not English. She grounds her book in the idea of the importance of teachers working collaboratively so "they possess more of an ownership to ensure positive results." She acknowledges that many teachers work with ELLs without professional support. Rather than just letting teachers languish with these circumstances, she has created a book that directly supports teachers and provides numerous ways for them to instruct their students in literacy learning.

The first chapter of her book suggests the importance of collaboration and provides ways for teachers to establish collaborative networks within their school. She doesn't just talk about the importance of collaboration; she offers practical suggestions of how to create these partnerships. Building from this chapter, she moves to a discussion of the importance of academic language, listening skills, and vocabulary. Her next chapter considers vocabulary and building background knowledge. She ends this book with connections to disciplinary-based learning.

The strength of Sasson's book is that she suggests practical ways to support ELLs. She moves beyond theory to the day-to-day expectations of classrooms. Her work suggests that teachers have high expectations for ELLs so that they can succeed in U.S. classrooms. In today's schools, a general-education teacher needs to understand how to work with ELL students in the classroom with or without ESL professional support (Barone & Xu, 2008). Her book does exactly that—it offers teachers numerous ways to instruct ELLs in language and literacy.

Diane Barone
University of Nevada, Reno

REFERENCES

Au, K. (2002). Multicultural factors and the effective instruction of students of diverse backgrounds. In A. E. Farstrup & S. J. Samuels (Eds.), *What research has to say about reading instruction* (3rd ed., pp. 392–413). Newark, DE: International Reading Association.

Barone, D., & Xu, S. (2008). *Literacy instruction for English Language Learners in the primary grades*. New York: Guilford Press.

Barone, D., & Morrow, L. M. (Eds.). (2003). *Literacy and young children: Research-based practices*. New York: Guilford.

Hadaway, N., Vardell, S., & Young, T. (2004). *What every teacher should know about English learners*. Boston: Pearson/Allyn & Bacon.

Neufeld, P., & Fitzgerald, J. (2001). Early English reading development: Latino English learners in the "low" reading group. *Research in the Teaching of English, 36*, 64–105.

Nieto, S. (1999). *The light in their eyes: Creating multicultural learning communities*. New York: Teachers College Press.

Xu, S. (2003). The learner, the teacher, the text, and the context: Sociocultural approaches to early literacy instruction for English language learners. In D. Barone & L. Morrow (Eds.), *Literacy and young children: Research-based practices* (pp. 61–82). New York: Guilford.

Preface

THE NEED FOR THIS BOOK

For more than a few years now, there has been a need for this kind of book. In today's day and age, a general-education teacher needs to understand how to work with ELL students in the classroom with or without ESL professional support, including the culture, the contextual factors of the school, and the legal underpinnings of dealing with ELL students.

With changing demographics and increased globalization worldwide, schools are at a crossroads in terms of how to reduce the achievement gap of K–12 ELL students across the country and especially at the secondary level. Teacher leaders most committed to social justice and inclusive practices (Theoharis, 2009) willingly work with their colleagues to enhance instruction for ELL populations and, in many cases, with little or no guidance or support from administration.

In the current economic climate of budget cuts and teacher job loss, teachers lack a system to support the academic needs and progress of their students and commitment to teacher leadership. Collaboration is now a tool for discussion, intervention, and support for ELL students before achievement gaps become too wide.

For the last few years, collaboration has been making strong ripples in the educational community. However, it is still not implemented in many districts and teachers are often discouraged from deviating from curriculum content. Clearly, there needs to be more support and time carved out for teachers to discuss concerns and plan lessons. In fact, research shows that teachers are more likely to outperform expectations and rise to the challenges when they are given the right conditions to collaborate.

Teachers across the country have already started to ride this "wave" by learning more of the positive benefits of collaboration for ELL students. Some teachers already are beginning to take matters in their own hands by dialoguing with other teachers in their schools to create the "ideal leadership" they envision for the twenty-first century. Others just starting their teaching careers need guidance and support in understanding how collaboration can ultimately benefit them and their students. Either way, it takes great faith, courage, and tenacity to begin and stick with a collaborative journey.

Now with the Common Core State Standards (CCSS) initiative, teachers and schools are challenged to implement the CCSS in English language arts (ELA) and mathematics with English language learners. Content-area teachers specifically need guidance as to how ELL students can meet these standards. To this end, school districts will need to provide necessary support for their ESL programs including a formalized ESL curriculum that needs to be established and aligned with the mainstream curriculum using the CCSS to help ELL students academically progress.

A solution to these challenges is in collaborative practices among ESL and content teachers, as well as co-taught classes. States like California, for example, have added about 15 percent more standards to those standards, making the need even greater to align content to standard. Teachers who work in a decentralized district will need to examine some of the instruction across content and decide how to share information. The need for collaboration for the sake of English language learners is now greater than ever.

THE INTENDED TARGET AUDIENCE FOR THIS BOOK

This book was written primarily for undergraduate and graduate students who either have or will have somewhere down the path of their teaching careers struggling readers who are also ELL students.

Secondary readership includes pre-service teachers or teachers in their first or second year of teaching with a specialization in ESL/ELL and/or early childhood. Veteran teachers who have taught mixed-ability groups and have students struggling with the reading foundations of acquiring a second language will also benefit from this book. Early childhood and preschool teachers working with struggling at-risk ELL students or lower-performing native speakers can also benefit from the information presented in this book as more and more ESL teachers are being asked to support pre-K and kindergarten and they need ideas for developmentally appropriate strategies.

Early intervention provides struggling ELL students and struggling readers the support they need in areas of reading and oral instruction. The intention of this book is to provide practical strategies and techniques grounded in theory to help teachers understand assessment, mapping, diagnosis, and various levels of reading proficiency before implementation. For teacher trainers, the information presented in this book can be used to differentiate various approaches for reading, decoding, and content-area literacy.

OTHER TARGET AUDIENCES AND USES

Each state has mandated objectives for pre-service teachers as well as opportunities to participate in professional development, which is also mandated by the district. Teachers involved in professional learning communities who use this resource as a "book study" that meet once a month for the purpose of increasing test scores and student achievement will find the book useful.

This book can also be used as a resource for ideas for Response to Interventions (RTI) teams or problem-solving teams (PST) that focus on student achievement.

Undergraduate students who teach in the primary grades would find this book helpful. It addresses collaboration and ELL methodology in a user-friendly text, with templates. There are lots of commonsense ideas for more than ELL students and especially for the lower-elementary student who learns visually.

Of course, all readers will benefit from wanting to collaborate more effectively in the instruction, teaching methods and strategies, planning, and assessment in order to better the academic needs of their struggling ELL students.

WHY THIS BOOK IS IMPORTANT

At the end of the day, a teacher wants to know: *How can I do my day better, more effectively to produce more positive results and outcomes despite my limited time and resources?*

This book takes the approach that even under the strictest time and curriculum constraints, teachers can start small by using one or more of the strategies and techniques listed in each of the chapters to help further a dialogue and increase awareness on collaboration.

The philosophy of this book centers on the idea that the power of collaboration begins with first seeing the "bigger picture." In fact, magic in the classroom can happen when two teachers who face a common problem can work together to find a solution. That bigger picture is formed when teachers start believing in the power of collaboration. When starting small, teachers can see the bigger road map of the journey.

This book was written to provide a starting point for that journey and to encourage teachers to use any of the tips or strategies presented here as a way to sensitize them to the value of collaboration and to encourage them to become better skilled at approaching situations with a collaborative eye for the sake of their own professional work and the achievement of their students.

REFERENCES

Teachers of English to Speakers of Other Languages. (1997). *ESL standards for pre-k–12 students*. Alexandria, VA: TESOL.

Theoharis, G. (2009). *The school leaders our children deserve: Seven keys to equity, social justice, and school reform*. New York: Teachers College Press.

Acknowledgments

Many, many thanks go out to all the teachers who spent much of their free time speaking to me about their experiences collaborating with other teachers for the sake of ELL students and sharing their resources for the benefit of other teachers. Their support has been invaluable from the start. A big, heartfelt thanks to my agent, Bertrand Linder, for believing in the vision of this book from the very beginning and helping me find a home for it. And a big shout of thanks to ELL teacher Kelly Grucelski, who offered invaluable feedback on the book's later drafts and helped make the pages shine.

Introduction

WHAT THIS BOOK DOES AND DOESN'T DO

This book was "born" from the premise that when teachers are part of the collaborative planning, they possess more of an ownership to ensure positive results. This book offers important background information on some of the most important challenges in supporting ELL students academically in various educational contexts and how teachers can use collaboration to address these needs and concerns.

In this book, you will learn how to use collaborative teaching practices to academically support your students in the skill sets of listening and reading. Both chapters take on an integrated skill approach also in the area of content. For example, the way listening has been understood and used in classrooms of ELL students is often taught isolatedly. Pre-listening activities have been predicated on the idea of activating prior knowledge. While listening activities are task-based and measure comprehension, post-listening activities usually consist of checking answers and moving quickly to a theme-related speaking activity.

However, listening can also provide an additional form of support in comprehension based on both the content and ESL teacher use. Similarly, collaborating in reading practices offers teachers a way to examine how to use read-alouds and reading strategies to complement speaking and listening and across content areas. In both chapters, you'll find descriptions and key concepts of various collaborative contexts for the benefit of English language learners.

Both chapters take an integrated approach to collaboration by maximizing language and cultural diversity in the classroom. ELL students enter classrooms with a variety of cultural backgrounds from formal schooling to prevailing cultural attitudes about group work and the role of the teacher.

Teachers need to learn all they can about providing language, literacy, and content to ELL students in diverse settings in order to prevent teacher isolation and gaps in quality instruction. Teachers new to collaboration for ELL students want to maximize their collaboration to provide the most effective instruction in *all* skill sets. If teachers want to emphasize collaboration as an essential skill for bringing about much-needed educational and social change, they need to maximize their own resources as much as possible. This book, therefore, focuses on the various collaborative models and configurations that will help guide teachers on this journey.

Getting ELL students to academically succeed requires a collaborative effort between the language professional and the regular education teacher. This implies that administration *must* be on board to support both endeavors. However, the complex issue of administrative support is *not* the focus of this book. The issue of administrative support varies from district to district and greatly depends on the quality of school leadership.

Not many teachers are able to fully enjoy the benefits of collaboration when an administration lacks the vision and leadership needed for collaboration to thrive. Therefore, rather than discuss what teachers should do to change the focus of school administrations for the benefit of collaboration, chapter 1 will discuss collaboration from a general perspective of school leadership.

Depending on state requirements, language and reading acquisition for ELL students and how their needs differ from native speakers may be the only information undergraduates get on second-language acquisition. In this respect, this book addresses several key areas pre-service and practicing teachers need to know as part of the second-language-acquisition process.

THE ORGANIZATION OF THIS BOOK

This book is grade specific and primarily targets the ELL population. The chapters are organized around skill sets and each chapter provides instructional strategies teachers can use to enhance their collaboration for the sake of academic progress in ELL students.

CHAPTER DESCRIPTIONS

Chapter 1 provides an overview on collaborative models and configurations, best practices for collaboration, the challenges and obstacles, the academic stakes behind collaboration, and a history of collaboration both past and present.

Chapter 2 provides strategies on how to scaffold academic language and content using the skill set of listening in the K–6 classroom. Various co-teaching situations and models will be explored.

Chapter 3 provides an understanding of the roles of English proficiency and English language proficiency, critical areas of co-teaching in early primary grades, as well as collaborating on targeted reading skills and standards. It also provides an overview of vocabulary and SLA influences, strategies for building background knowledge, and other schemata. Various co-teaching situations and models will be explored.

Chapter 4 provides strategies and techniques for collaborating in the areas of content literacy as it relates to a read-aloud curriculum as well as techniques that support K–6 ELL students learning how to read, differentiation techniques, and explicit academic teaching of vocabulary. Various co-teaching situations and models will be explored.

THE PURPOSE

There are several purposes of this book, including:

- to define academic language development and academic content in the context of team-teaching on K–6 levels;
- to explore how teacher collaboration and co-teaching can provide an effective platform for integrating language, literacy, and content from kindergarten to grade 6;
- to address how teachers can collaborate to make content instruction comprehensible to ELL students at the various levels of language proficiency;
- to show how collaborative practices can support the continuum of academic language development along with reading comprehension, speaking, and writing;
- to show how collaborative practices can support the challenges of supporting reading comprehension at the K–2 and 3–6 levels using real-life scenarios;
- to define teacher collaboration, collaborative team-teaching, and co-teaching in the context of academic support for ELL students; and
- to establish a vehicle for professional development toward creative collaboration between ESL and general-education teachers.

HOW TO USE THIS BOOK

Each chapter focuses on collaborative practices of co-teaching with specialists including the ESL and reading teacher to support reading, speaking, and writing in an academic context as well as both formal and informal collaborative practices. The chapters are structured in a similar fashion for consistency. Recurring features are intended to provide easy access to the content of the book.

Overview: Each chapter begins with a descriptive preview by emphasizing the key ideas.

Chapter questions: With the exception of chapter 1, each chapter starts with two to four questions based on research principles of a key issue of language learning and teaching that supports collaboration.

Best practices in the classroom: Each chapter includes several authentic classroom and teacher snapshots designed to show collaboration in action and how co-teachers were able to bring the skill and/or strategy to life.

Summary: At the conclusion of each chapter, there are brief recaps of the main ideas and their implications for teaching and collaboration.

Study group discussion questions: Chapters 2 and 4 provide critical-thinking questions designed to take the understanding to a higher level.

Activities for further collaboration: Each chapter provides opportunities to discuss the topic in more detail, applying the ideas to an everyday practical scenario.

Web sources: Chapters 2 and 4 include a series of content-related links that provide an extension of some of the topics addressed.

TERMINOLOGY USED IN THIS BOOK: A NOTE ON ESL AND ELL TERMINOLOGY

In this book, the abbreviation *ELL* will be used as all inclusive regardless of the type of program or grade level—specifically, *ELL* will be referred to as an ELL student or students to avoid generic labeling. Although there are many different ways to refer to an ELL student's level of proficiency in English, in this book the levels developed by Teachers of English to Speakers of Other Languages (TESOL) will be used: level 1—starting; level 2—emerging; level 3—developing; level 4—expanding; and level 5—bridging. Such standards guide teachers in establishing the knowledge and skills their students need to acquire. Teachers can use these standards to write goals stating what they want their students to know at the end of a lesson or unit of instruction.

To talk about an ELL's native language, the term *L1* will be used, and to talk about his/her second or additional language, English, the term *L2* subsequently will be used.

To date, regarding the current educational settings of ELL students, there is also a need to distinguish between an ESL support group and a general-education classroom as well as the collaborative contexts for ELLs as either English as a second language (ESL) or general education (GE).

ESL is an older term that has fallen out of favor because some students may be learning English as their third language. *ELL* (English language learner) is now the preferred term. However, for purposes of identifying collaborative roles and responsibilities in conjunction with the general-education and content-area teachers, the term *ESL teacher* will be used to refer to the language professionals and the ELL students as those children who work directly with an ESL teacher and as the same students in the general-education or mainstream classrooms.

Chapter One

Introduction to Collaboration for K–6 English Language Learners

In the past, the focus of collaboration was on the needs of special-education students in general-education classrooms. In today's academic environment, collaborating for the sake of ELL students is a "must" if teachers want to close academic gaps in content-area literacy in ELL students from kindergarten. Enhancing collaborative partnerships benefits all involved in the process. However, there are still limited opportunities in today's academic environment for all who are involved in the teaching of ELL students to collaborate, leaving teachers to work on their own or seek collaborative resources outside the district.

Teachers continue to face ongoing challenges with time, money, and issues of school leadership that often get in the way of effective collaboration. However, in the long run, teacher collaboration may yield the most effective instruction to meet the diverse academic and language development needs of ELL students. This chapter will focus on the history of collaboration, obstacles, and the various models that are currently being used in today's classrooms to build collaboration and knowledge.

In this chapter, the following topics will be covered:

- an introduction to the different collaborative practices and co-teaching arrangements, promising practices that are emerging as a result of teacher collaboration such as instructional and non-instructional collaborative practices among ESL and mainstream teachers; and
- a history of collaboration and how it has been used in the special-education classroom.

HISTORY OF COLLABORATION—PAST AND PRESENT

Dorit Sasson was an ESL teacher and Tracie Heskett was a general-education teacher in the same school. Both teachers had considerable numbers of ELL students in their class. Meeting the diverse needs of Tracie's ELL students meant constantly finding interesting and successful ways to keep them on task. Dorit needed to ensure that her struggling ELLs were also acquiring word/text-based skills in an ESL context.

The common thread that links both Dorit and Tracie's work is in instructing struggling ELL students—some of whom study with both teachers. In Tracie's general-education class, there were several ELL students. In Dorit's ESL class, the emphasis was on learning the language. Both teachers had some common planning time to interact professionally to discover the best approaches to working with struggling ELL students in both educational settings, thus allowing them to build partnerships. This type of relationship most represents the general picture and classroom reality of many teachers in schools across the nation.

COLLABORATION—PAST AND PRESENT

Historically, special-needs children in the United States were not part of the regular educational day, and moreover, regular education and special education teachers did not collaborate. Before 1997, the law did not include a regular education teacher as a required member of the Individualized Education Program (IEP) team. Under the 1997 Individuals with Disabilities Education Act, the IEP team for each child with a disability now must include at least one of the child's regular education teachers if the child is or may be participating in the regular education environment. The new law also states that the regular education teacher, to the extent appropriate, participates in the development, review, and revision of the child's IEP.

As can be seen with English language learners, collaborating for the sake of special education students implies that special education students would receive support, instruction, and educational standards from regular education teachers. In this respect, collaboration between special-education teachers and regular education teachers can take different approaches. Some special-education students have a team of educators, instructors, therapists, and specialists working with them to guarantee the most successful results. These students may be in a regular education classroom with a regular education teacher for most of the day and then get pulled out of the room for a few hours to complete work with a special-education teacher.

Other students may have a special-education teacher in the regular education classroom with them, working closely with the regular education teacher in a sort of co-teaching model. Similarly to English language learners, the special-education teacher generally modifies the curriculum of the classroom to best support the special-education student, sometimes pulling him out to a quiet area to read or take a test, sometimes spending extra time with him to complete assignments, and often modifying work to meet the requirements of the student's IEP.

PRESENT-DAY COLLABORATION FOR ELL STUDENTS

In today's educational environment, the same collaborative framework used for special-education students also exists for teachers of ELL students. Collaboration is mainly implemented in school districts that have access to resources and funding to support collaborative practices and various pilot programs.

If teachers are to collaborate effectively for the sake of ELL students in today's academic environment, rigorous guidelines and policies need to be implemented and funding must be appropriated. Committees must meet to discuss academic outcomes. In order to place ELL students on an equal playing field for future learning and continued growth that will allow them to compete in an ever-changing and technological world, general-education and other specialized teachers must collaborate. The topic of collaboration needs to be put on national agendas.

While the No Child Left Behind Act (2001) opened a door for rethinking how to diversify teaching methods, learned practices, and materials so that they appeal to a wide variety of learning styles and abilities typical of many ELL classrooms today, teachers still need guidelines in place to support ELL students' academic progress and achievement. This can only work if there is administrative and national support for collaboration to take place.

Collaboration for the sake of special-education students was recognized for one main reason: teachers worked together to fulfill the requirements of an IEP around inclusion-based issues of students of special needs in general-education classrooms. Fulfilling the rigorous requirements of an IEP requires an in-depth knowledge of the curriculum as teachers provide academic, emotional, and social support of special-education students in general-education classrooms. School districts continue to work with administrators and teachers to implement various models and educational frameworks to support the instructional delivery of these students. For the sake of collaboration, teachers are expected to cover a great deal of academic content in diverse classroom settings while they are also expected to integrate ELL students academically.

WHY TEACHERS MUST COLLABORATE

If collaborative frameworks accommodate the rate by which ELL students are absorbed into the general-education classrooms and the degree to which they are expected to understand content-area texts, ELL students would have a greater chance at academic success. Some demographic projections show that 40 percent of the school-age population in the United States will be ELL students by the year 2030 (NWREL, 2004).

Research shows that English language learners represent the fastest-growing student group in U.S. schools, with enrollment increasing more than 150 percent since 1990 (NCELA, 2006). This will put more pressure on teachers to account for students' academic progress. In many cases, ELL students show up in regular education classes and it falls on general-education teachers to provide almost all instruction, sometimes with the aid of an ESL professional, but many times without.

This ongoing increase has impacted the way in which national ELL experts and educators view ELL proficiency and how they view the relationship between academic language and content. A blog post on *Education Week* (August 16, 2011) reaffirms that national ELL experts and educators are working toward a new direction whereby they are leaving behind the assumption that standards alone guide teachers in establishing what knowledge and skills their students need to acquire, and are currently creating a framework of the English-language demands within the Common Core standards for Math and English language arts, as well as for the National Research Council's next-generation science standards.

Between now and the end of 2013, a team of teachers and researchers will analyze the academic language required in different content areas and develop an open-source platform of resources to help teachers of English language learners implement the new standards. Kenji Hakuta, who is spearheading the project, states, "We're not trying to develop standards per se, but we are trying to call attention to the fact that language undergirds much of instruction and learning for all students and especially for English learners. We need to be very aware of the language basis for academic content" (para. 7).

Projections indicate that in two decades, this demographic group will comprise more than one-third of students in U.S. schools. Yet the drop-out rate continues to grow. An important implication for collaboration that is emerging from these new developments confirms the need for teachers to define as part of their planning how academic language goals will be met based on ELL students' proficiency in academic language of a specific content area and the extent to which teachers integrate a balanced instructional approach in their collaboration.

Enhancing collaborative partnerships benefits all students, teachers, and the school community. However, obstacles such as money, time, and school leadership continue to pose a problem to all stakeholders involved in the academic success for ELL students.

OBSTACLES TO COLLABORATION

So why isn't collaboration being implemented in all school districts that have English language learners—even in those districts that have a small number of ELL students? The three biggest reasons are:

- resources and funds,
- school leadership, and
- curriculum and time constraints.

The Problem of Funds and Other Resources

Currently, when states are cutting funds for K–12 programs as well as higher education, administrators tend to think that collaboration between teachers is an expense they cannot afford. In today's academic learning environment, money has become an excuse for hiring and firing teachers as well as curtailing expenses, resources, funding, and other programs.

School Leadership: Coping with the Classroom Realities of Time and Curriculum Constraints

Time Constraints

One of the assumed goals of collaboration for special-education students is that teachers work to better meet the academic needs of their students. However, in order to involve all the stakeholders, schools require appropriate funds, resources, and time for teachers to collaborate. The ESL teacher alone does not have the time to teach all the required content-area vocabulary students need for success! If schools, for example, want ELL students to be on an equal playing field alongside native English speakers, they must invest in pilot-based collaboration-based programs with tailored agendas to meet academic needs.

Lack of time is a reality of classroom life. However, school leaders also need to recognize the importance for teachers to be able to interact with each other on a weekly or daily basis to discuss students' needs and for teachers to plan together. Equally important is scheduling time for administrators and teachers to meet together. In light of this situation, leadership time and funding are all inextricably connected when it comes to support collaboration.

In the article "The Missing Link in School Reform" (2011), Carrie R. Leana states that principals are more successful in producing achievement gains when they focus on providing resources to help teachers build connections as opposed to mentoring and monitoring teachers. If administrators and principals invest in "social capital" (para. 4), or the qualities of building trust and closeness and learning from their conversations with others, teachers will become better in their field of expertise.

True reform efforts happen when trust and meaningful communication among teachers lead to frequent discussions around areas of instruction that ELL students seem to struggle with the most. Based on the results from the survey distributed to more than 1,500 kindergarten to fifth-grade New York City teachers, Leana notes, "If a teacher's social capital was just one standard deviation higher than the average, her students' math scores increased by 5.7 percent" (para. 19).

In a district-wide context that supports collaboration, teachers are given *time* to collaborate. Honigsfeld and Dove (2010) equate a strong administration who believes in collaboration with positive school culture and "play a critical role in providing the human and material resources necessary for teacher collaboration and co-teaching practices to develop and thrive" (p. 139).

For example, a special-education and ESL teacher can discuss a co-teaching plan by sharing with the administration some of the problems and creative solutions for finding time to collaborate. Teachers can share the frustrations of not having a planning-hour block to sit with a crew of special-education teachers and intervention specialists so they can benefit from additional instructional support.

Finally, school leadership influences the degree to which teachers and other stakeholders develop partnerships. If ESL teachers and general-education teachers do not have opportunities for professional interaction, the relationship between ESL and general-education teachers may not lend itself to support and collaboration. For instance, the ESL teacher might come into the general-education classroom to help, but may be made to feel like a teacher's aide. Or the ELL students might be separate in another classroom, where they may or may not be learning the same curriculum as their native peers.

Classroom Constraints

Another classroom reality is that of curriculum constraints. In many school districts, teachers are mandated to use a particular curriculum. Administrators in many school districts discourage deviation from the curriculum content so that teachers can cover the required skills. If ELL students do not have the background knowledge and skills, teachers cannot be expected to speed up the curriculum at the expense of the instruction of ELL students.

WHAT ARE THE CONSEQUENCES OF NOT COLLABORATING?

In today's age of collaboration for ELL students, there are many stakeholders of ELL students who require time and resources to collaborate in the planning, instruction, and assessment of ELL students. These include:

- ESL and content teachers;
- ESL and bilingual teachers;
- ESL and resource teachers;
- ESL and classroom/mainstream teachers;
- ESL and special-education teachers;
- ESL program, school, and district administrators; and
- ESL program and curriculum coordinators.

Lack of adequate time or the resources to collaborate will lead teachers and other stakeholders to figure out on their own the best way to academically support ELL students across the content areas. One of the long-term consequences that occur as a result of a lack of support is that schools placed on the Adequate Yearly Progress (AYP) are listed for subgroups not meeting growth in specific learning areas that require content-based instruction of reading comprehension and vocabulary. Consequently, these schools are also targeted for not meeting the same levels of growth other student groups are either meeting or exceeding.

ELL students tend to be one of those cultural groups that may end up on this list that determines the amount of funding allocated to them on a federal level and based on No Child Left Behind (2001). The fact that ELL students are not reaching the required reading standards and proficiency calls for additional funding. As a cultural subgroup, ELL students may continue to not meet the same levels of growth because they are constantly targeted. In doing so, they become a statistic and are never completely supported within a school's system. Inevitably, it becomes the teacher's job to find ways to help them succeed academically.

Increasing numbers of struggling ELL students are not reaching academic proficiency by the end of the fourth grade. These learners are later associated with special needs and slow learners, learning-disabled learners, as well as ADHD and ADD learners. In light of this issue, frameworks for collaboration must be in place for the sake of young ELL students in order to support them academically in all content areas of learning.

SUPPORTING K–2 ELL STUDENTS

On a K–2 level of instruction, academic achievement for ELL students implies incorporating language/literacy skills. Since the nature of the demands of reading change over time, monolingual English students need a balanced form of literacy to address literacy as well as language to help them deal with text. Conversely, teachers need co-teaching strategies to emphasize meaning-making in reading and writing by incorporating more language-rich and literacy-rich activities that support academic development across the content areas.

Collaboration in the areas of literacy, language, and content for K–2 ELL students requires:

- knowledge of effective oral reading instruction that promotes vocabulary knowledge and phonological-awareness training;
- knowledge of the decoding process so learners can make connections between ideas while reading; and
- knowledge of effective fluency strategies that at-risk and struggling ELL students need early on in the decoding process.

COLLABORATIVE MODELS FOR ELL STUDENTS

In today's educational world, teachers are put under tremendous pressure to speed up the curriculum at all costs and for all students. In an age of increased accountability and standardized assessments, a collaborative model supports teachers' work within constraints of the curriculum. Collaborative models, which are a system of guidelines usually given to teachers by administration such as team teaching or parallel teaching, can help English language learners succeed academically if teachers integrate literacy, language, and content (Calderon, Slavin, & Sanchez, 2011).

Similar to the inclusion-based setting of special-education students and students of special needs where a team of teachers is responsible for the delivery of instruction and assessment, likewise, team teachers of ELL students will need to make constant modifications and adjustments in the general-education classroom. Recognizing the types of problems and understanding how these models can best cater to the unique needs of ELL students is the first step to effective collaboration.

The alarming increase of special needs and number of referrals to specialized schools has also paved the way for a greater number of co-teaching or team-teaching classrooms (Malka, 2011). However, collaborative models still need to be integrated in general-education classrooms even where there are a few English language learners. Many of these inclusive classrooms are often staffed by a general-education teacher who spends many hours alone in instructional planning, classroom management, and assessment. These teachers are the best candidates for a supportive ESL co-teaching framework.

USING AN ESL CO-TEACHING FRAMEWORK

Recognizing the value and expertise of an ESL teacher is central to the idea that a partnership between ESL and content-area teachers can impact academic achievement of ELL students. Multiple models of instructional practice in co-teaching have been recommended by Cook and Friend (1995). For some teachers, co-teaching may not be an option if there is no ESL teacher onsite or if teachers lack the necessary preparation for effectively educating this group.

Tracie Heskett, a second-grade general-education teacher, started the school year with several ELL students only to learn there was no ESL specialist onsite. However, she was able to learn from the experiences of other teachers at school and how they worked with their ELL students.

However, in many school districts, one common model that is currently used is the ESL co-teaching model.

Calderon (2011) proposes five main purposes of an ESL co-teaching framework:

- to address the same theme, genre, essential questions, standards, key vocabulary, and reading and writing skills, and building background information and reviewing key concepts;
- to joint plan, which means allocating school time for joint planning;

- to co-develop complementary lessons or materials;
- to map and align the curriculum; and
- to collaboratively assess student work and plan next interventions.

Clara Lee Brown (2005) refers to this kind of interactive onsite support as "direct consulting," where general-education teachers apply their knowledge of the subject-area curriculum and instruction, while the ESL teacher provides knowledge on second-language acquisition issues and teaching strategies (para. 7). As suggested by Calderon (2011), a supportive ESL co-teaching framework provides opportunities for ELL students to be included in aural-oral activities so they can develop academic language skills throughout their schooling years.

In a supportive ESL co-teaching framework, a first-grade teacher, for example, observes a special-education teacher who teaches several groups of students with special needs including ELL students. The special-education teacher becomes familiar with the role of the first-grade teacher through a hands-on experience by supporting and assisting. Together, they enjoy a hands-on learning experience, by sharing materials and planning collectively with a colleague who is equally invested in the students' achievement.

Co-teaching requires introspection, self-questioning, as well as a variety of intrapersonal and communicative skills and strategies including a willingness to not only hear but also truly listen to the other side and be able to effectively verbalize one's professional needs, wants, and goals. First-grade teacher Tara Malka (2011) agrees: "Co-teachers who recognize each other's strengths and capitalize on them are ensuring that their students meet their personalized educational goals" (para. 9).

In a co-teaching environment, teachers are able to cater to the learning needs of ELL students in the following ways:

1. Both teachers direct the class and are in front of the class. The general-education or core teacher teaches content while the ESL teacher provides examples, clarifies, uses visuals, restates, etc.
2. Teachers switch roles 50 percent of class time. The core teacher teaches, and the ESL teacher monitors or assesses students, and then they switch roles.
3. The class is divided in half and both teach the same content to a heterogeneous group. Both teachers are knowledgeable in the areas of teaching vocabulary, reading-comprehension skills, and writing specific to a content area.
4. Turn-taking. The ESL teacher pre-teaches vocabulary while the core teacher presents the concepts. The ESL teacher asks/clarifies questions, elicits summaries from students, and reinforces the use of new vocabulary.

5. Switching. Both teachers teach multiple groups by switching groups every twenty minutes or so.

As teachers become proficient in the various models, they can plan to use a variety of them. The concept or the skill being covered and students' learning styles will inform the model that works best. The following four models described in detail include:

Model #1: Team Teaching

Regardless of the program type or grade level, team teaching can help ELL students achieve academic outcomes. This model consists of both teachers teaching the same students at the same time. Teachers ensure ELL students have success by the quality of instruction, continuous professional development, whole-school structures, and effective leadership that institutes team teaching (Calderon, 2011).

Both co-teachers work together and actively share the planning and instruction of content and skills to all students. Both teach the material by exchanging and discussing ideas and concepts in front of learners, facilitate small-group work and student-led discussion, and model appropriate ways of asking questions. For example, one teacher might talk while the other teacher models a read-aloud or writes on a whiteboard.

Benefits of Team Teaching

- Like other models, teachers work closely to reach solutions to issues relating to students such as behavior, motivation, and teaching styles.
- Both teachers have the opportunity to teach all students.
- Additionally, it provides a supportive environment for both teachers and students.

To meet the needs of ELL students using this type of intervention, the general-education teacher prepares special material and activities for ELL students who are still in small groups or are in general-education classes. The material and activities will be on the same subject matter and include some of the same curriculum goals as regular classroom instruction. However, they will be geared to potentially at-risk or struggling students. The content-area or general-education teacher can collaborate with the ESL teacher in preparing such special activities and materials.

There are various configurations that allow maximum collaboration in a team-teaching setup:

- ESL teachers team with general-education teachers.
- RTI tier-2 teachers team up with tier-1 teachers.
- ESL teachers team up with special-education teachers (or RTI tier 3).
- ESL teachers team up with general-education and special-education teachers.

In a co-taught model, teams of teachers also work collaboratively in the same classroom to plan and implement the interventions and share progress-monitoring and data analysis.

Model #2: Additional Structures for Team Teaching: Push In or Pull Out

Push in and pull out are organizational models that support team teaching configurations. There are many classroom environments where general-education teachers do not have the privilege of working with an ESL specialist.

In schools where there is an ESL specialist, ELL students are mainly "pulled out" of general-education classrooms for special instruction in English as a second language. This, however, creates significant stress on the ESL teacher to perform. As Pardini (2006) and Zehr (2011) note, unless teachers have successful cooperative planning and organizational techniques to work in teams, the "pull-out" organization will not help close the language gap for the sake of ELL students. For this reason, more teachers across the country are moving away from the "pull-out" model.

Support for Push In

Even though more districts are pulling away from pull-out configurations, the debate continues. Unfortunately, there is no conclusive research on the effectiveness of supporting the relationship between academic gains and proficiency levels. However, there is an added cultural and social advantage when ELL students study with their native English-speaking peers.

As pointed out by Nicole Fernandez, a second-grade ESL teacher who taught in a pull-out context before moving to a push-in: "It has been a challenge for administration to see the positive effects of this program. However, the students have had a positive effect. The ESL students say they like it so much better. They are not lost in class anymore. The general-education students are much more culturally aware and have gained new relationships."

Teachers in this school district reported they were able to coordinate interventions and pre-teaching so ELL students would not experience random instructional events when the school district moved to the push-in model.

Models #3 and 4: Parallel Teaching and Group Models

Two co-teaching models in particular lend themselves to the delivery of scientific-research-based interventions—parallel teaching and the group model.

Parallel Teaching

If a large number of ELL students in a class require the same intervention, the *parallel teaching* model may be best. This model is most effective when there is a need to differentiate reading materials and provide extension activities to one group while re-teaching another group. In this model, one educator delivers the intervention to one group, while the other educator delivers instruction to the other group. The group receiving instruction could be expanding on concepts already learned, reviewing, or using the time for self-selected reading. Groups can be formed according to reading level or learning styles.

Benefits of Parallel Teaching

- The student-teacher ratio is low.
- Students have more opportunities to get help and support.
- Students' responses and knowledge can be more closely monitored.

Large Group/Small Group

When a small number of students in a class need the same intervention, the large-group/small-group model may be best. In this model, one teacher works with a small group (two to five students) who need the intervention, while the other teacher continues instruction with the larger group. This model is used to either re-teach a learning concept or extend learning for a group of students. The main importance is to keep groupings as flexible as possible when transitioning from activity to activity.

This model also works best when implementing intervention with an individual student. Using this model requires much more planning than the parallel model, because the intervention must fit into a time in the day or class period when students can move in and out of the larger group without missing new instruction. A benefit to this model is that it can be used when teachers find it necessary to progress and monitor students.

Benefits

- Teachers have additional instructional time to support struggling students.
- Teachers can provide more individualized instruction and, therefore, build a learning and educational profile of each student.

COLLABORATION ON A WHOLE-SCHOOL STRUCTURE

Many district ESL directors offer some professional development, but these development courses are not always subject-specific and ongoing to the needs of ELL students. To support collaboration for the sake of ELL students, professional development must help all teachers understand second-language acquisition and be able to incorporate new strategies and methodologies including the opportunity to co-teach to improve instruction for ELL students.

ESL program models, collaborative models and roles, teamwork, and structures should frame continuous professional development. Instituting professional development occurs through administrative support, which is the backbone for whole-school support (Calderon, 2011).

For English language learners, the cost of covering the curriculum is greater than usual, as teachers often inadvertently ignore the language needs of these students in content courses. Calderon (2011) recommends that schools strategize and maximize professional development to include all teachers involved in the teaching of ELL students regardless of grade level, subject area, language of instruction, and educational contexts, as revealed in the following examples:

- three–five initial days of professional development where ESL and content teachers participate by grade levels to address specific needs of teachers: kindergarten to grade 8 and ninth- through twelfth-grade cohorts;
- professional development in English and professional development in first language (e.g., Spanish) for bilingual classrooms; and
- refresher workshops during the year for all teachers on all components and as needed.

THE ROLE OF ADMINISTRATION IN CO-TEACHING AND COLLABORATION

Calderon, Slavin, and Sanchez (2011) offer the following eight features to ensure academic success:

- providing time for planning time/collaboration between general-education and ESL teachers;
- scheduling ESL teachers' workload with care;
- grouping ELL students by proficiency levels and no more than two grade levels;
- keeping ESL classes small (below fifteen; ideally ten);

- one ESL teacher per content area (one for math, one for science, etc.);
- providing all necessary resources and materials;
- providing ongoing professional development for general and ESL teachers together; and
- promoting high status for all ELL efforts and respect for team teachers.

Administrative support can also impact the degree to which teachers and many members of staff are engaged in peer coaching and teacher support. For example, coaches and site administrators participate in training for ELL students. General-education and ESL teachers attend workshops on peer coaching and coach each other to improve instruction and learning. Co-teachers observe and document student performance and their co-teacher's instructional delivery. Peers record observations of ELL students or co-teachers.

WHAT DO DIVERSITY STANDARDS IMPLY FOR COLLABORATION?

Since English language learners are also a K–12 issue, teachers need to know how to provide culturally and linguistically responsive instruction that is viewed and addressed as a part of K–12 education. Associations such as the National Association for Bilingual Education (NABE) and the National Council of Accreditation for Teacher Education (NCATE) place special emphasis on providing "on-grade-level" academic knowledge and skills, which include literacy at the elementary and secondary levels to bilingual learners.

In 2010, the NABE drafted a national action for the education of bilingual learners. The last forty years of research on second-language acquisition in the United States has affirmed the effectiveness of using a child's native language to learn academic concepts while learning the English language. However, schools have yet to catch up with the research, leaving teachers to cope with a consistently growing academic achievement gap between native English speakers and bilingual learners.

A great deal of diversity exists in how schools help teachers approach bilingual learners, as indicated by the Standards for Reading Professionals (International Reading Association, 2010) and how schools create a diverse environment for collaboration to flourish and grow. One of the assumptions implies collaborating for the sake of providing culturally and linguistically responsive instruction across educational contexts. It identifies the fact that "language-minority students need appropriate and different language and literacy instruction if they are to be successful academically while they learn English" (2010).

Similarly, in 2008, standard four of six teacher-education standards developed by the NCATE focused on diversity. For teachers, this means they provide equal access to an academic and linguistic education to help ELL students become "English proficient" and academically on grade level. It states, "experiences provided for candidates include working with diverse populations, including higher education and P–12 school faculty, candidates, and students in P–12 schools" (2008).

By coming together in their cultural understandings of their diverse learners and deliberately incorporating these conversations in their collaboration, teachers can meet the instructional standards of diversity. Curran (2003) describes that "when teachers learn to see the diverse backgrounds of their students as resources, these students' experiences can serve to promote the multilingualism and multiculturalism of all the students and the teacher" (p. 338).

WORKING WITH LEARNING DISABILITIES IN A COLLABORATIVE CONTEXT

Similarly to those collaborative models that presently serve general-education and special-education teachers for the sake of students with special needs, teachers of ELL students need to be supported in their work with ELL students who may have a learning disability.

In fact, the number of ELL students with learning disabilities has risen so much in many districts that the need for developing strong, collaborative relationships with ESL and bilingual teachers as well as special-education professionals and specialists has become that much more acute. Shah states (2011), "With some states experiencing a 700 percent growth in the number of English learners in their schools between 1994 and 2005, the department expects the number of English Learners with disabilities to increase, too" (para. 1).

However, the problems understanding the issue require knowledge of second-language acquisition and effective interventions. In some districts that do work with ELL students with learning disabilities, a collaborative framework helps teachers facilitate communication in their collaboration. Finding solutions to learning disabilities is challenging especially when teachers have to take into consideration a language barrier, which can complicate the situation (Santos & Ostrosky, n.d.).

When teachers and specialists refer an ELL student to special-education services, is the problem always a learning disability, or is it a second-language acquisition issue? How does intervention play a role in collaboration?

Would the special-education support be the kind of help that student needs? How can teachers effectively collaborate for the benefit of these students?

There are no easy answers to these questions. A common thread that emerges from these difficult questions reinforces the need for enhanced communication and cooperation among all teachers who share the responsibility of teaching ELL students who may exhibit signs of a learning disability with the specific target of maximizing what Allington refers to as "instructional expertise" (2011, p. 173).

In many cases ELL students who have learning disabilities often do not receive the services they need. Their problems may go unrecognized because they are second-language learners. They may be referred to special education but not receive appropriate services because of a lack of bilingual special-education teachers. They are not assessed for learning disabilities because of their lack of English.

Before teachers move too quickly in the direction of special-education referrals, districts need to improve the quality of teacher training for general-education teachers who work with an increasingly diverse student population including English language learners, children from diverse cultural backgrounds, and children living in poverty to help bring awareness and sensitivity to the many variables such as poverty, stress at home, or upheaval due to the immigration process and moving to a new country with a different culture. Additionally, schools can improve general-education strategies by implementing teacher teams to improve instruction that is data driven, collaborative, and includes schoolwide intervention as well as appropriate language support in teams.

THE INCLUSION MODEL

Inclusion is the best response to the idea that, to the maximum extent possible, students with disabilities are to be educated with their nondisabled peers in the general-education classroom. Whether catering to ELL students or special-needs students in an inclusion-based environment, teachers use their knowledge of co-teaching to help them expand their teaching to include the broadest range of learners.

The inclusion model assumes that all students, regardless of ability, level, or background, will receive research-based, high-quality, differentiated instruction from a general-education teacher in a general-education setting. The objective of differentiated instruction is to maximize each student's growth and teaching from that point. The underlying view of differentiated instruction is that "one size does not fit all"—an idea counter to an assumption in many classrooms.

Routinely, the general educator assesses students' progress in the curriculum and makes ongoing adjustment to target the needs of students including those with special needs and English language learners.

CREATING A CO-TEACHING MODEL FOR ELL/LEARNING-DISABLED STUDENTS

Whether co-teachers are instructing ELL students who may be learning disabled or instructing students of special needs in an inclusion-based setting, both special-education teachers and ESL/content teachers will need to work collaboratively in the same classroom to deliver instruction. This collaboration involves jointly developing and agreeing upon a set of common goals, sharing responsibility of obtaining these goals, and working together to achieve these goals using each others' expertise.

ESL Team Teaching

ESL teacher-led teach teams is one way for all teachers of ELL students to discuss language, literacy, and content in an inclusion-based setting. For the delivery of special-education and related services, teachers are encouraged to use a team approach whenever possible led by the ESL teacher in the position as a "direct consultant" (Brown, 2005, para. 9). Where other professionals would directly benefit from her/his expertise including students who need special-education and language support services and allows for team planning to collaborate with bilingual/ESL personnel.

Teacher teams include general-education and special-education teachers, paraprofessionals, and building specialists who design the intervention plan at different tiers to discuss the role of second-language acquisition issues and ESL strategies for co-teaching. The problem, however, that teachers continue to face is that the kind of support given to students with reading or language disabilities is not the kind of support that second-language learners need, which, again, reinforces the need for enhanced communication and collaboration among all teachers who share the responsibility of teaching these kinds of ELL students.

When it comes to referring either a struggling or at-risk elementary ELL student to special services or interventions, the expertise of an ESL teacher on the issues of second-language acquisition can be most useful in determining possible treatments. One common cause for referral of these students has to do with misinterpreting the area of error analysis made by second-language learners.

Ellis (2003) raises important points for distinguishing between errors and mistakes. Equally important for teachers to consider is the learner's stage of second-language acquisition particularly regarding a learner's silent period, a developmental pattern where the learner is deeply absorbing the language but is not producing it—largely a feature in communicative settings. In many cases where the "silent period may serve as a preparation for subsequent production" (p. 20), teachers can start the process of classifying grammatical errors early "as a way to help us *diagnose learners' learning problems* at any one stage of their development and, also, to plot how changes in error patterns occur over time" (p. 18).

For example, leaving words out in speech or in writing is an example of the early stages of L2 acquisition. But if these errors persisted in the intermediate stages of second-language learning, teachers may need to evaluate the level of consistency in the learner's performance versus possessing knowledge of the correct form or whether the learner was just slipping up a mistake random to a specific area of producing language in communication.

Since second-language acquisition is largely an internal process, much also has to do with mother-tongue interference. As Rod Ellis (2003) states, "Some errors are common only to learners who share the same mother tongue or whose mother tongue manifests the same linguistic property" (p. 19).

Understanding what learners do when exposed to the L2 in communicative settings reveals a great deal of the level of second-language acquisition and what the ESL and general-education teacher can do to further collaboration:

- diagnosing errors in terms of type, frequency of occurrence, and
- distinguishing passive vs. active production—from a second-language-acquisition point of view, since many struggling ELLs who exhibit silent behaviors are silent.

To develop an intervention plan that provides struggling readers with more intensive instructional support, teachers need to maximize each teachers' "expertise" and a "decreased classroom size" (Allington, 2011) in order to increase the likelihood of reading acceleration. For the sake of effective collaboration, teachers need to follow specific guidelines to make these interventions effective for second-language learners. Although Allington's principles of intervention refer to struggling readers whose mother tongue is English, all professionals need to provide ELL students who have reading or language disabilities with customized support.

SUMMARY

It is only recently that teacher collaboration for the sake of English language learners is gathering more attention from the educational community. In today's era of high academic stakes and standardized testing, collaboration for the sake of English language learners is necessary for teacher and student academic success. Collaboration creates a supportive learning environment for teachers and for students. When teachers collaborate frequently and consistently, they are able to optimize the learning environments as they continue to cope with ongoing challenges.

REFERENCES

Allington, R. L. A. (2011). *What really matters for struggling readers: Designing research-based programs.* Boston: Allyn & Bacon.

August, D., & Shanahan, T. (Eds.). (2006). *Developing literacy in second-language learners: Report of the National Literacy panel on language-minority children and youth.* Mahwah, NJ: Erlbaum.

Barone, Diane. (2008, December 8). "Someone I'd Like You to Meet: Professor Diane M. Barone." Interview. *New Teacher Resource Center.* Retrieved December 8, 2008, from http://newteacherresourcecenter.com/?p=537

Brown, C. L., & Bentley, M. (2004). "ELLs: Children left behind in science class." *Academic Exchange Quarterly, 8*(3), 152–157.

Brown, C. L. (2005). "Ways to help ELLs: ESL teachers as consultants." *Academic Exchange Quarterly.* Retrieved December 20, 2010, from http://findarticles.com/p/articles/mi_hb3325/is_4_9/ai_n29236331

Calderon, M. E. (2007). *Teaching reading to English language learners, grades 6–12: A framework for improving achievement in the content areas.* Thousand Oaks, CA: Corwin.

Calderon, M. E., & Minyana-Rowe, L. (2011). *Preventing long-term English language learners: Transforming schools to meet core standards.* Thousand Oaks, CA: Corwin.

Calderon, M. E., Slavin, R. E., & Sanchez, M. (2011). Effective instruction for English language learners. In M. Tienda & R. Haskins (Eds.), *The future of immigrant children.* Washington, DC: Brookings Institute/Princeton University.

Cook, L., & Friend, M. (1995). Co-teaching: Guidelines for creating effective practices. *Focus on Exceptional Children, 28*(3), 1–16.

Curran, M. E. (2003). Linguistic diversity and classroom management. *Theory into Practice, 42*(4), 334–340.

Ellis, R. (2003). *Second language acquisition.* Oxford: Oxford University Press.

Honigsfeld, A., & Dove, M. (2010). *Collaboration and co-teaching: Strategies for English learners.* Thousand Oaks, CA: Corwin.

International Reading Association. (2010). Standards 2010: Standard 4. Retrieved June 6, 2013, from http://reading.org/General/CurrentResearch/Standards/ProfesionalStandards2010/ProfessionalStandards2010_Standard4.aspx

Leana, C. (2011). *The Missing link in school reform*. Stanford Social innovation Review. Retrieved September 1, 2011, from www.ssireview.org/articles/entry/the_missing_link_in_school_reform

Malka, T. (2011, April 14). *Exploring methods of effective co-teaching*. United Federation of Teachers. Retrieved September 6, 2011, from www.uft.org/teacher-teacher/exploring-methods-effective-co-teaching

National Association for Bilingual Education. (2010). National action plan for the education of bilingual learners. Retrieved July 25, 2011, from www.nabe.org/files/NABE_NATIONAL_ACTION_PLANS.pdf

National Clearinghouse for English Language Acquisition. (2006). *The growing number of limited English proficient students 1991–2002*. Washington, DC: U.S. Department of Education.

National Council of Accreditation for Teacher Education. (2008). Six teacher education standards. Retrieved July 23, 2011, from www.ncate.org/Standards

Northwest Regional Educational Laboratory. (2004). ELL unit focuses on growing population. NW Report.

Office of English Language Acquisition. (2003). Descriptive study of services to LEP students and LEP students with disabilities. University of Minnesota, National Center on Educational Outcomes. Retrieved June 6, 2013, from www.ncela.gwu.edu/files/rcd/BE021199/special_ed4.pdf

Pardini, P. (2006). In one voice: Mainstream and ELL teachers work side-by-side in the classroom teaching language through content. *Journal of Staff Development, 27*(4), 20–25.

Santos, R. M., & Ostrosky, M. M. (n.d.). Understanding the impact of language differences on classroom behavior. What Works Brief no. 2. Nashville, TN: Center on the Social and Emotional Foundations for Early Learning. Retrieved June 6, 2013, from http://csefel.vanderbilt.edu/briefs/wwb2.pdf

Shah, Nirvi. (2011). More English Language learners, more ELLs with disabilities? Retrieved July 13, 2011, from http://blogs.edweek.org/edweek/speced/2011/08/_the_us_department_of.html

Teachers of English to Speakers of Other Languages. (2007). ESL standards for pre-K–12 students. Retrieved December 17, 2008, from www.tesol.org/s_tesol/seccss.asp?CID=95&DID=1565

U.S. Department of Education. (2006). 28th annual report to Congress on the implementation on the *Individuals with Disabilities Education Act*, vol. 1. Retrieved June 6, 2013, from www2.ed.gov/about/reports/annual/osep/2006/parts-b-c/28th-vol-1.doc

Zehr, Mary A. (2011). Stanford to lead creation of ELL standards for "Common Core." Retrieved July 12, 2011, from http://blogs.edweek.org/edweek/learning-the-language/2011/07/stanford_to_lead_creation_of_e.html?qs=hakuta

Chapter Two

Collaboration in the Development of Listening Skills

I received my class list at the beginning of the school year and identified one third of my students as English language learners. At the time I didn't know these students' capabilities, but it seemed likely that some of them would struggle with reading. Our school didn't have an ESL specialist on staff and I knew I would need help to meet the academic needs of my students. Dorit Sasson suggested collaboration with other teachers in the building, as well as our online collaboration.

—Tracie Heskett, a second-grade general-education teacher

INTRODUCTION: WHAT ARE THE MOST COMMON PROBLEMS ELL STUDENTS EXPERIENCE?

Research shows that the most common problem ELL students experience is understanding the meaning of academic texts. As ELL students acquire more academic vocabulary across content areas, teachers need to ensure that ELL students make important literary and deeper comprehension connections. At all emerging stages of literacy, listening provides the framework for second-language instructions and builds the academic language of ELL students before they are expected to read.

This chapter begins by addressing the role of listening in K–6 ELL students. Next, it defines academic language and goes on to identify a number of effective and practical ways to co-teach and promote academic language in content areas. It also considers some characteristics of effective listening instruction and promising practices for content instruction comprehension using listening instruction. The chapter concludes with identifying language objectives in listening.

CHAPTER QUESTIONS

- What is the role of listening instruction in vocabulary development and reading comprehension across content areas and what is the implication for collaboration?
- What are some ways to promote listening activities in co-teaching contexts?
- What elements of oral academic language instruction should teachers consider when co-teaching and supporting struggling ELL students?

DEVELOPING LISTENING TO IMPROVE READING FLUENCY AND COMPREHENSION

Closing the achievement gap for ELL students requires significant understanding of how vocabulary and academic language affect reading comprehension. The importance of developing listening proficiency is a building block in developing reading and writing skills for ELL students. Good listening habits will lead to better academic language competence. English language learners in both general-education and ESL settings are immersed in instructional and non-instructional settings where they hear and understand oral language daily.

While these English language learners are proficient in understanding social language, which is generally informal, and is primarily used to communicate with family members and friends and others in everyday social situations, research supports the need for students to acquire listening and textual fluency and comprehension skills simultaneously (Bailey & Heritage, 2008). At the critical stages of K–2 instruction, teachers need to make sure that struggling ELLs can make connections between oral and written forms of words.

Broersma and Cutler (2008) discuss how non-native students of English use their first-language listening strategies to listen in their second language. They routinely rely on native-language word stress (in English, usually the first syllable). Native speakers of English know where words begin and end because of reliable cues; for example, an English word cannot begin with [bw], but in some Arab dialects words can begin that way. "So learners have difficulties recognizing words in the speech stream and they have difficulties suppressing wrong guesses because they cannot suppress L1 cues" (Brown, 2011).

UNDERSTANDING THE ROLE OF LISTENING INSTRUCTION IN VOCABULARY DEVELOPMENT

A big problem that starts from early literacy is that students often have been taught vocabulary words in reading class. They have no idea how the words sound when spoken. They might have heard the word a couple of times, but most practice has been written. Therefore, teachers need to develop in their students across content areas a robust and aural vocabulary.

In this respect, a math aspect of word recognition is vocabulary. If ELL students can work with cues and recognize words, they need to know the meanings of those words. The size of students' vocabulary is one predictor of academic success. "Vocabulary is the single, strongest predictor of academic success for second language students" (Kinsella & Feldman, 2005).

Collaborative instruction in this respect can help teachers scaffold or "break down" the sounds of new academic and non-academic words and terminology across content areas and for all grade levels. To increase more opportunities to use listening in academic learning contexts, teachers need to extensively use a combination of *academic talk*, which is verbal classroom interaction addressing focal lesson content, framed in complete sentences with appropriate vocabulary, syntax, grammar, and register" (Kinsella, 2007) and deliberate activities such as dictation and dicto-comp and dicto-gloss.

THE BENEFIT OF COLLABORATING ON DICTATIONS

By adopting some old tried-and-true methods like dictation, teachers can focus on some ongoing problems facing ELL students when it comes to recognizing words. Dictation is also beneficial when it comes to targeting academic words in a content area and then practicing them in an academic or non-academic context. Collaborating in the area of dictation is a good first place to start. There are several outstanding educational and learning benefits.

Dictation relies on multiple modalities—listening, writing, reading—and is perfect for multilevel classes. Dictation works by storing information in a student's working memory and reproducing it in chunks. Much of the current research on second-language acquisition is concerned with constructions, chunking and memory. Dictation, therefore, is a perfect learning solution in today's classrooms of ELL students.

The easier way to use dictation in a collaborative setting can work in one of two ways:

1. The class is divided in half and both teachers teach the same content to a heterogeneous group. Both the ESL and content teacher are well skilled in sheltering content (teaching listening) to a specific area. In this way, each teacher focuses on the pronunciation of targeted vocabulary and/or marks the stressed areas of each vocabulary word to facilitate the L2 cues needed for comprehension and understanding especially when students will later see these words in context. This preliminary instruction would also strengthen the aural instruction of the words prior to dictation.
2. The same procedure in #1 is used with a whole class when both teachers are directing the class and are in front of the class. In this respect, the core-content teacher focuses on the academic and/or nonacademic meanings of targeted vocabulary words while the ESL teacher provides visuals to emphasize the pronunciation, stress, syllabic construction, and collocations.

Given the difficulties in capturing the correct pronunciation of targeted vocabulary, there is great merit in using dictations that ask students to put minimal pair words with similar stress into columns.

Types of Noncommunicative Dictations

Teachers can consider reading a short text that is slightly different from the one students have. Lower-ability students can cross out words that are different from the teacher's while higher-ability students write the correct word.

Other Communicative Dictations

1. The teacher reads a text. Students write what the teacher says, but add their personal information. For example, "I was walking down the street and saw _____." Students work in pairs to read their stories.
2. The teacher holds up a picture, says true/false things about it. Students write only things that are true. Higher-ability students put the sentences into T/F columns.

COLLABORATING ON PRONUNCIATION IN COLLOCATIONS

Nation (1991) points out that dictation focuses on phrase and clause construct, and on collocations, which are expressions composed of two or more words typically used together to express a certain meaning. The focus in teaching these collocations would be helpful in illustrating how substituting one of the individual words in the following expressions such as "a hardened criminal," "to run a business," or "to crash a computer" would break the usual form of the collocation and thus alter the meaning.

From an academic teaching standpoint, collocations also represent an opportunity for teachers to integrate phrasal clusters and idiomatic expressions along with reading and listening instruction, which fall in the category of tier 2. Calderon (2011) also suggests using the concept of *tiers* to select and deliberately teach academic content-specific words to ELL students and struggling readers.

Tier 2 words may be simple enough for English speakers to pronounce and understand, but might create difficulty for ELL students due to pronunciation. In co-teaching configurations, the ESL and content/general-education teacher have many opportunities to integrate vocabulary and listening in a content-based lesson.

Examples:

run off
run away
break a leg
once in a while
complete sentences
long noun phrases
relatively easier
stored energy
stimulus package

Sample Collaborative Scenario Using "Turn-taking" to Teach Tier 2 Words

Prior to a lesson, both teachers select words from a tier 2 vocabulary list to teach struggling readers and ELL students. The ESL teacher pre-teaches vocabulary. The core teacher presents a short reading text with the targeted words either underlined or in bold. The ESL teacher asks/clarifies questions and reinforces the pronunciation of targeted vocabulary and/or marks the stressed areas of each vocabulary word to facilitate the L2 cues needed for comprehension and understanding. This preliminary instruction would also strengthen the aural instruction prior to comprehending these words in a short expository text.

USING LISTENING TO SUPPORT MEANING OF VOCABULARY IN TEXTS

ELL students who have limited English proficiency in general-education classes often have difficulty making academic connections. "Young children, especially those at risk, benefit from nurturing, robust early learning environments that expose them to rich language and many words" (Roskos et al., 2001). Struggling ELL students need opportunities to hear words orally to help them increase comprehension and give them the foundation to develop reading and comprehension skills.

ELL students who have not yet acquired, by the end of the second grade, enough academic language to understand "academic texts" or texts that contain academic terminology of school will often hypothesize meaning in an attempt to interpret the message of oral and written input. Therefore, if co-teachers wish to improve the reading proficiency of their struggling ELL students, they also need to consider the ways listening in the form of "academic talk" (Kinsella, 2007) can support the development in ELL students of hearing words and their synonyms and antonyms as well as opportunities for imitation.

Best Practices in the Classroom

In a science class consisting of only ELL students at the Partnership Academy, a charter school of 270 students with 90 percent receiving some kind of ELL service just outside St. Paul, Minnesota, fifth-grade teacher Kelly Grucelski introduces and clarifies new vocabulary of different types of rocks using hand formations. She says:

- "Hands together means that the volcano is exploding. This is an example of an igneous rock." [She models the appropriate hand formation and study and repeat—same goes for the others.]
- "Hands on top of each other means a sedimentary rock or the layers of rock formation."
- "Pushing your hands together indicates a metamorphic rock, which shows the rock is under heat and pressure."

As a follow-up to each of these examples, teachers can state: "Hands together means that the _____ is exploding," and ask students to provide the missing word and the corresponding hand formation. In this way, providing abundant opportunities for listening helps ELL students "comprehend and develop concepts in ways they would not be able to do on their own" (Levine & McCloskey, 2008, p. 20).

SECOND-LANGUAGE ACQUISITION: HOW DOES THE INPUT HYPOTHESIS SUPPORT INSTRUCTION?

Most classroom teachers are not informed about practices used to help ELL students in the classroom (Lewis-Moreno, 2007). Based on responses to a recent survey, general-education teachers feel that an understanding of language acquisition will improve their knowledge of supporting ELL students' proficiency and academic progress.

From the end of grade 2, the input hypothesis plays a crucial role as ELL students are expected to read for understanding and learning across subject areas. To implement the input hypothesis, co-teachers need to recognize the principle that ELL students must understand the communication of their teachers. Language is not "soaked up."

One way teachers can meet this ongoing need is by weaving listening when using instructions and explanations to make explicit connections between written and spoken words, as revealed in the example on page 28. To make progress in the target language, second-language learners need to understand input (either speech or written text) that is a little more complex than the language they are currently able to produce (i + 1) but it must be comprehensible. Stephen Krashen refers to comprehensible input as the "most important of any language teaching program" (Krashen & Terrell, 1983, p. 55).

Managing comprehensible input requires teachers to also make content more comprehensible. One of the ways to do this is by helping ELL students negotiate meaning. As teachers rotate between subject areas, in many cases, they may encounter a need to reinforce specific concepts and language structures by making strategies more comprehensible, as illustrated in textbox 2.1.

Lori D. Oczkus (2010) suggests that reinforcing verbal responses to students' understanding of a text is one way to focus on comprehension. From the third grade, teachers need to help ELL students negotiate meaning in all their learning experiences as they acquire academic content knowledge and vocabulary.

Teaching ELL students to negotiate meaning requires supporting them through form and meaning. A good language learner will often shift between form and meaning. The lower the reading proficiency, the more an ELL will attend to meaning. By managing comprehensible input, teachers help ELL students negotiate meaning and therefore facilitate the acquisition process.

For example, teachers can discuss modification strategies to help ELL students learn at higher levels (otherwise known as scaffolding) by selecting various types of physical and visual support to provide background knowledge before ELL students learn new academic content. The higher the proficiency, the more learners will attend to form. The lower the proficiency,

TEXTBOX 2.1.
Strategies to Help Make Content Comprehensible for ELL Students

ELL students have linguistic and cultural issues that often get in the way of academic vocabulary acquisition. Even though second language acquisition is dependent on a formal process, teachers can modify their oral speech to provide more comprehensible input. Students do not always "get" new content the first time.

1. Slow down the rate of speech.
2. Use simple sentences whenever possible.
3. Explain the same concept multiple times in various ways.
4. Provide visual aids including pictures, diagrams, charts, graphic organizers, regalia, and hands-on activities to support conceptual understanding.
5. Provide extensive scaffolding at all stages of second language development. Since ELL students do not have the same background knowledge as native English speakers, teachers need to point out certain concepts in the lesson that need to be visualized and scaffolded.
6. Identify language for complex concepts that need to be simplified.
7. Act out vocabulary so students can internalize the meaning of the words.
8. As students read, have them make hand motions and gestures to remember parts of the story as an aid to building visual memory.
9. Have picture dictionaries available as a resource so students can see the words within sentences.
10. Connect the understanding of individual words within sentences. ELL students do not often hear these types of endings. Helping them understand the grammatical structure of a word will also assist with the comprehension of word parts and phrases.
11. Ask students to restate the vocabulary and content in their own words.
12. Provide clear enunciation of targeted vocabulary.

the more difficult it will be for learners to pay attention to different things happening simultaneously in the reading process.

Questions of Form

Would the meaning of this word (or groups of words) change if the word was somewhere else? Would the pronunciation and/or meaning of this word (or groups of words) change if the stress were somewhere else?

Question of Meaning

What does this word mean in the context?

To sum up, providing comprehensible input (Krashen's hypothesis) can ensure comprehension by doing the following:

- When teaching academic vocabulary, bridge listening and reading formats. An ELL student acquires a *listening vocabulary* prior to recognizing words in context. Students need explicit vocabulary instruction, not just exposure, taking into account that they need twelve production opportunities to own a word.

USING THE CONSULTING MODEL TO SUPPORT THE SKILL OF LISTENING

After consulting with the ESL teacher, general-education teachers may do one or more of the following:

1. present reading skills and concepts in smaller segments;
2. use visual diagrams to accompany explanations and to scaffold difficult concepts and ideas in order to strengthen students' understanding of concepts presented in class;
3. monitor the use of talking;
4. provide more listening activities that can meet the academic and language development needs of ELL students; and
5. use listening activities to differentiate between exposure and practice. For example, students are exposed to new vocabulary when they hear the word or read-aloud or text for the first time. They experience practice when they make connections between the written and oral forms of the words.

In addition, there are listening goals teachers can evaluate at the end of each quarter. *By the end of the _____ quarter, students will be able to . . .*

- understand oral clues or prompts when teacher explains assignments;
- understand English orally in various contexts such as read-alouds, songs, spoken texts and narratives, interviews, and dialogues;
- construct a response where they are expected to write answers or solve and explain problems;
- understand new vocabulary words orally and in sentence context;
- pronounce tier 1/2/3 words after recognizing their stresses, sound blends, and collocations on word or sentence levels;
- recognize sound blends and sounds on word, sound, or sentence levels.

Table 2.1 is a tool teachers can use to make students' goals more attainable, especially in the area of listening, which is hard for teachers to ascertain since listening is an internal process. Teachers can consider the scaffolding needed in terms of how to achieve their goals and objectives. This table, of course, can be adapted to suit the learning needs of all four skills.

Table 2.1. Assessing a Needs Analysis in the Area of *Listening*

Name of Student	Concepts and/or Skills Student Still Needs to Know or Learn to Complete Necessary Tasks	Types of Necessary Skills Needed to Pre-teach for Understanding	How Big Is the Gap between Current and Desired Performance?*

*For purposes of measuring the learning gap, teachers can use the following elements of a sliding scale: "substantially below grade level," "borderline range," and "satisfactory progress."

A SAMPLE LISTENING ASSESSMENT FOR EARLY PRIMARY GRADES

The most commonly administered informal needs assessment is a "get to know you" that pre-assesses what students know in an informal learning situation.

Assessments in listening are often overlooked. Although it can be challenging to get a full, complete picture of students' listening abilities, such assessments can be invaluable in helping teachers understand how ELL students acquire language. This type of informal assessment is typically administered at the beginning of the school year, and then students are reassessed periodically as they acquire more English.

Part of the objective of this pre-assessment is to evaluate if ELL students could recognize the words orally and to see how well they were able to understand the words in both an oral and print context. In many cases, they perform much better when they are read the words aloud.

The two-part activity below supports listening cues of isolated words and words in context. Most standardized test questions rely on students' reading knowledge and do not explicitly test active listening skills.

Part 1: Getting to Know Each Other

1. Put a check next to each word you can read.
2. Circle each word if you know what the word means.
3. Draw a line between two words that relate to each other in some way.

pizza _____	basketball _____	computer _____
school _____	color _____	language _____
English _____	books _____	sports _____

Now, listen to your teacher read the words to you.

How many words did you get right? _____

Conclusions

Most likely, if students recognized the meanings of these words, they would be able to make connections between the written versions of these words spoken orally. In some scenarios, maybe all ELL students would be able to sound out the words and a few ELL students would be able to understand some of the words. For purposes of this exercise, ELL students may require explicit instruction that would enable them to recognize these meanings when they are heard orally.

The next exercise promotes active listening and word recognition based on the words from the previous exercise. Teachers can start by reading the passage slowly, sentence by sentence, stressing a random word in each sentence. The students circle each word teachers stressed.

Getting to Know Each Other Part 2: Lee Wong and You

Lee Wong is a new student. He speaks Chinese and English. He plays basketball with his friends. He plays computer games and reads scary books. He loves sports.
   Lee cooks dinner. He makes a pizza. "Pizza is my favorite food!" he says.

Now, listen as your teacher tells you which words you should have circled.

How many words did you get right? _____

IDENTIFYING LANGUAGE OBJECTIVES IN LISTENING

Time and curriculum constraints make it virtually impossible for an ESL teacher to teach all the necessary levels of academic and content knowledge an ELL student needs while focusing on active listening skills. For example, if an ESL teacher has only forty-five minutes to sixty minutes a day with a group of students, how can that teacher teach all those words in and out of context? ELL students need to master five or more words per subject area every day and three thousand to five thousand academic words a year.

Therefore, collaborating on content and language objectives facilitates the process of helping ELL students meet that content objective in English. Not all ELL students will be developmentally ready to use these language structures in their speaking and writing.

Once teachers know their content objective (what they want students to be able to do), they can identify the language ELL students would need to know to be able to meet that content objective in English. On the tier 1 level, teachers focus on the basic words ELL students need to communicate, read, and write—those that need to be taught. Using tables 2.2, 2.3, and 2.4, teachers can complete the column that pertains to listening and then use this information to determine how much time to set aside in a given lesson to reinforce pronunciation and collocations as well as how to integrate listening with reading.

Table 2.2. (Tier 1) Main Language Structures (or Grammatical Components)

	Speaking	Reading	Writing	Listening
ESL related				
General content area #1_____				
General content area #2_____				
General content area #3_____				

Table 2.3. Academic Language: (Tier 2 and 3) Content-Specific Vocabulary

What content-specific vocabulary will ELL students need to understand and use in reading, speaking, listening, and writing?

	Speaking	Reading	Writing	Listening
ESL related				
General content area #1_____				
General content area #2_____				
General content area #3_____				

Table 2.4. (Tier 3) General Academic Words

This category refers to the general academic words ELL students will need to complete academic tasks. These are words that are used across many subject areas and in various contexts (e.g., *identify, compare, process, describe, analyze, benefit*).

	Speaking	Reading	Writing	Listening
ESL related				
General content area #1_____				
General content area #2_____				
General content area #3_____				
General content area #4_____				

In addition to content-specific vocabulary words, academic language also includes many general academic words and is often more abstract.

> **TEXTBOX 2.2.**
> **Ways Teachers Can Use Speaking and Listening at All Stages of the Reading Process**
>
> **Linguistic Support**
>
> - **Paraphrase** academic language in the text using everyday language and ask students to report back.
> - Add key vocabulary words from a text to a word wall or a chart and **discuss** their meanings with students.
> - **Examine** how the language is used in the text to understand its meaning. This is a good time to point out tricky language structures (e.g., signal words, referents, verb tenses, nominal phrases).
> - During **guided reading**, pay attention to which vocabulary words or language structures each ELL student has difficulty reading and comprehending. **Discuss** these aspects of the language when you regroup the students to talk about the text. This can also be done with individual ELL students during reading conferences.
> - **Model** question starters and language prompts that ELL students can use to talk about their text when the process of comprehension breaks down (e.g., "What does ____ mean?" "**I don't** understand this part." "How do I ____?" "**Would you** please repeat that?" "Could you explain it to me?")
>
> **Visual Support**
>
> - Point to illustrations or diagrams when reading a text to help explain the meaning of vocabulary words or sentences or to stress pronunciation or collocation.

A Step-by-Step Recap of Collaboration between ESL and General Education/Content Teachers (This Can Be Applied to All Four Skills)

1. Take a critical-needs analysis of students.
2. Evaluate the results of pre-assessments and assessments.
3. Decide which areas of instruction are most needed based on respective curriculum.
4. Analyze specific areas of instruction to meet the needs of struggling readers. If applicable, teachers can analyze which particular critical areas overlap both general-education and ESL curriculums.

5. Map or strategically identify various categories of student difficulty according to benchmarks and standards.
6. Consult with the ESL teacher on appropriate teaching and differentiation strategies and assessments.

CHAPTER SUMMARY

To develop listening skills, teachers of ELL students need to go beyond comprehension to work on the areas of speech. This is not to say that comprehension in academic and nonacademic contexts should be ignored but to say that instruction should not be limited to comprehension exclusively. Providing embedded listening activities such as dictations in reading-based contexts provides an integrative approach to teaching academic and nonacademic vocabulary.

This chapter illustrates the importance of building a dialogue around what general-education teachers already know about their students and how to incorporate more opportunities for listening activities. Attention to active listening skills leads to better academic language competence. The collaborative examples provide a "thinking platform" for planning and teaching listening that can support academic language for ELL students in the general-education classroom.

During the intermediate stages of second-language acquisition, collaborating for the sake of integrating listening with reading instruction requires understanding the unique role of listening in second-language acquisition. Teachers consider ELL students to be at risk when they struggle with language-learning issues, as evidenced by difficulty with several specific areas of phonetic and decoding skills and later word and sentence recognition.

Struggling students need additional listening support to develop skills and content knowledge in accordance with national standards; TESOL has compiled standards specifically for ESL students designed to bring these students to a level at which they can meet national academic standards.

WEB SOURCES

Many links and content-area English language teaching strategies including SIOP, CALLA, and GLAD: www.oswego.org/webpages/lstevens/index.cfm?subpage=8246

"Teaching Language through Content" from CAL (Center for Applied Linguistics): www.cal.org/resources/archive/rgos/content.html

Oral diagnostic assessments for ELL students: www.suite101.com/content/oral-diagnostic-assessments-for-ells-a146279

"Fluency Building Strategies Using Easier Texts": http://doritsasson.suite101.com/fluency-building-strategies-using-easier-texts-a86466

STUDY GROUP DISCUSSION QUESTIONS

1. Many teachers across the country are concerned about the level of instruction they are providing to ELL students and if it is enough for students' academic needs. What do you consider to be "enough" in terms of helping ELL students make academic progress? How does the skill of listening enter this picture? How does collaboration enter this picture?
2. According to research on secondary-language acquisition and fluency, teachers can facilitate fluency when ELL students are provided with easier texts where 99 percent of academic vocabulary is understood. The more challenging the text, therefore, the less motivated an English language learner will be to understand it.
3. Reflect on a recent text you gave your ELL students. Was this text easy or difficult for your ELL students to understand? What areas of vocabulary and text support did they need help with the most? Try to isolate them. Decide how you can facilitate meaning and comprehension by focusing on one of the following areas: pronunciation, collocations, stressing individual words.
4. Brainstorm a list of teaching challenges in listening and possible solutions with another teacher. What areas were most common? How would collaboration facilitate this area of instruction?

The questions below are intended to stimulate and encourage teachers to think about working in collaborative contexts:

1. In which areas have you already experienced some success with co-teaching?
2. How do you think co-teaching can help you support listening skills in your ELL students? What is your main priority in teaching your ELL students? What do you see as the critical teaching goals?
3. How do you see co-teaching helping with the process of addressing the role of listening in your struggling ELL students?
4. What language structures emerge as more common to both ESL and general content areas?
5. What content-specific vocabulary emerges as more common to both ESL and general content areas?

ACTIVITIES FOR FURTHER COLLABORATION

1. Pool a group of students from a class or an entire class you are currently teaching. Identify areas in listening that need short- and long-term solutions to meet the needs of students.
2. Identify strengths and resources of each teacher in your collaborating group. Use this information to help you plan lessons and generate a wide range of activities for targeted skills.
3. With a co-teacher, identify ways to group students based on language and academic skills using ELL students' listening abilities.
4. From the beginning of the school year, collaborating teachers need a system in place to cope with ongoing time and curriculum constraints. Pre-planning listening activities and lessons is one way for teachers to overcome this. Set aside short blocks of time for thirty minutes at the beginning or end of the school day or during parts of a lunch break. Have a focused agenda of one to two doable points. Put this system to the test. What works? What doesn't? What needs improvement?
5. Begin a collaborative notebook where you keep notes about a particular class and their performance on listening-based tasks. Make notes about student performance during collaborative activity for academic instruction. How did the students respond to the collaboration? What was easier for you and them? You can also use this information to inform your collaboration for activity #4.
6. Brainstorm a list of time-management and self-management strategies to help you determine how much time is needed for a particular listening activity.
7. Brainstorm a list of concerns you may have about supporting ELL students in the area of listening. What will your ELL students need to succeed in your class? More background knowledge? Additional linguistic and visual support?
8. An important aspect of the collaborative process is evaluation. Teachers need to reflect on their experiences and ask themselves questions to obtain the greatest benefit. The answers to these questions will help teachers plan further collaboration. Use a success or reflective journal for this purpose.

SUGGESTED READING

Ellis, Rod. (2003). *Second Language Acquisition*. Oxford: Oxford University Press.

REFERENCES

Bailey, A. L. & Heritage, M. (2008). *Formative assessment for literacy, grades K–6: Building reading and academic language skills across the curriculum.* Thousand Oaks, CA: Sage/Corwin Press.

Beck, I. L., McKeown, M. G., & Kucan, L. (2002). *Bringing words to life: Robust vocabulary instruction.* New York: Guilford Press.

Broersma, M., & Cutler, A. (2008). Phantom word recognition in L2. *System, 36,* 22–34.

Brown, S. (2011). *Listening myths: Applying second language research to classroom teaching.* Ann Arbor: University of Michigan Press.

Calderon, M. (2011). *Teaching reading to English language learners in K–5th grades.* Online course, Solution Tree Press.

Calderon, M. E., August, D., Slavin, R. E., Cheung, C. K. A., Duran, O., & Madden, N. A. (2005). Bringing words to life in classrooms with English language learners. In A. Hiebelt & M. Kamil (Eds.), *Research and practice on vocabulary* (pp. 115–136). Mahwah, NJ: Lawrence Erlbaum.

Kinsella, K. (February 17, 2007). Academic language development presentation for Mountain View School District. El Monte, CA.

Kinsella, K., & Feldman, K. (2005). *Structures for active participation and learning.* New York: Scholastic Red.

Krashen, S. D., & Terrell, T. D. (1983). *The natural approach: Language acquisition in the classroom.* Hayward, CA: Alemany Press.

Levine, L. N., & McCloskey, M. L. (2008) *Teaching learners of English in mainstream classrooms (K–8).* Boston: Pearson.

Lewis-Moreno, B. (2007). Shared responsibility: Achieving success with English Language Learners. *Phi Delta Kappan, 88*(10), 772–775.

Nation, P. (1991). Dictation, dictocomp, and related techniques. *English Language Teaching Forum 29,* 12–14.

Oczkus, L. D. (2010). *Reciprocal teaching at work: Powerful strategies and lessons for improving reading comprehension* (2nd ed). Newark, DE: International Reading Association.

Roskos, K. A., Tabors, P. O., & Lenhart, L. A. (2001) *Oral language and early literacy in preschool.* Newark, DE: International Reading Association.

Teaching children to read: An evidence-based assessment of the scientific research literature on reading and its implications for reading instruction. *National Reading Panel.* 2006. Washington, DC: NICHD.

Chapter Three

Collaboration in the Development of Reading Skills

The challenges of academically supporting ELL students in reading are common to many classrooms across the nation, and testify to the fact that they cannot always do the same work as native English speakers without additional scaffolding instruction and content. Acquiring reading skills at the same time as acquiring English language skills is a complicated process for all levels of ELL students and there are numerous opportunities to co-teach and collaborate by integrating vocabulary and language progressions. In the middle elementary stages, teachers need to ensure they are teaching a comprehensive approach to reading in the four core subjects of language arts, social studies, math, and science for academic success.

When ELL students do not have access to enough academic vocabulary and content knowledge, they struggle with understanding academic texts. This situation creates even more challenges for teachers who already differentiate and target academic language for each proficiency level and range of schooling background. It is also not effective for the ESL teacher to teach all the required content words and vocabulary ELL students need for academic success. With effective planning and team teaching, however, both content and ESL teachers can support ELL students' progress through the different proficiency levels.

This chapter explores the complexities of the reading needs of K–6 ELL students and provides a clear profile of how collaboration and co-teaching can address and support these needs. This chapter begins by describing the role of English proficiency and English language proficiency in collaboration and co-teaching in the area of reading. Next, it defines critical areas of co-teaching and provides co-teaching scenarios of struggling ELL students.

It then explores a number of effective and practical ways to collaborate in the area of targeted reading skills and standards and general collaborative planning strategies. It also considers some of the second-language acquisition theories that relate to ELL students' unique struggles with acquiring vocabulary and language and the implications for collaboration. Finally, it describes how co-teachers can monitor areas of quality reading instruction and how ELL students acquire comprehension skills.

QUESTIONS

- What is the difference between English proficiency and English language proficiency and how can they help with collaboration?
- What are some theories of language acquisition researchers have identified as important in second-language acquisition? What are some of the implications of these theories for collaboration?
- What are some ways teachers can co-teach in the critical areas of reading instruction?

HOW CAN UNDERSTANDING THE ROLES OF ENGLISH PROFICIENCY AND ENGLISH LANGUAGE PROFICIENCY HELP WITH COLLABORATION?

To effectively support K–2 ELL students in the early stages of learning to read, co-teachers need to be aware of the differences between English proficiency and English language proficiency and its role in early literacy development. While TESOL (2007) has developed goals and standards to provide educators with starting points of English language proficiency to ensure that students who come from non-English-speaking backgrounds progress in accordance with national academic standards, educators of ELL students can benefit from a clearer distinction of English proficiency and English language proficiency as they support their ELL students through the different proficiency levels.

For both terms, reading is comprehension. However, the difference between English proficiency and English language proficiency depends on the degree to which ELL students, and particularly those in K–2 settings, fully comprehend what they read.

According to Snow et al. (1998), English proficiency is equated with progress in the area of learning to read in English beyond the initial level along with sufficient practice to achieve fluency, or automaticity, with different texts.

Teachers of struggling ELL students, for example, need to provide effective reading instruction to help promote vocabulary knowledge, phonological awareness training, and other basic reading skills so that these students can automatically process and fluently read more complicated and challenging academic texts.

In a co-teaching ESL framework, an ESL teacher's area of expertise lies within the knowledge of language-acquisition theory while literacy or reading knowledge is not the strongest area for many ESL teachers. To this end, language-acquisition theories help to explain the process by which a second-language learner acquires a second language to strengthen the reading process. In a collaborative context, therefore, ESL teachers can benefit from the expertise of a reading or literacy specialist (and vice versa).

In such a partnership, this type of information can therefore strengthen the pedagogical support of how both a reading specialist and an ESL teacher can co-teach struggling ELLs in the general-education class using the knowledge of language-acquisition theories to support fluency and automatic processing theories.

Moreover, at all stages of language learning and acquisition, assessing English language learners can also help with the process of supporting English proficiency and English language proficiency. Assessing English language learners for various areas of English language learning helps ascertain how well ELL students are progressing. The teacher's reading checklist in textbox 3.1 describes the various levels and degrees of struggle of English language proficiency in the critical early years of learning how to read.

ESL and reading and literacy specialists/teachers, for example, can use this checklist to discuss targeted areas for practice and help ELL students move from limited language proficiency to English proficiency in the content areas. Teachers can use parts or all of these components to determine the struggling ELL students in their classes. They can follow up by responding to the corresponding assessment link questions.

Best Practices in the Classroom: Co-planning

For each grade level at the Partnership Academy school, there are two general-education teachers and one ELL teacher—a total of six ELL teachers in all. Kelly Grucelski works together with the fifth-grade content-area teachers. They have 1.5 hours of planning time for a two-hour reading block. The ELL students, some of whom read on a third-grade level, stay in their homeroom groups. For the first hour, she co-teaches with the literacy/reading specialists with one group and for the second hour, she works with vocabulary and spelling with the other group.

Every Thursday, they decide who is going to prepare the components and presentation materials as well as independent work for two hours of literacy.

TEXTBOX 3.1.
An ESL and Reading Specialist Checklist:
Identifying Struggling ELL Students

Decoding Level: Student Experiences One or More of the Following Difficulties

- Decoding one-syllable words
- Identifying vowel sounds, diphthongs, consonant blends, number of phonemes (sounds) in a word, vowel diagraphs (e.g., ow, ou, ei)

Basic Reading Level: Student Experiences One or More of the Following Difficulties

- Reading basic sight words
- Reading basic words associated with grade-appropriate concepts (parts of the body, transportation, food) as well as words students hear and read in stories and informational texts

Sentence Level: Student Experiences One or More of the Following Difficulties

- Comprehending one or more words in context
- Comprehending the entire sentence

Text Level: Student Experiences One or More of the Following Difficulties

- Retelling the main idea
- Making inferences
- Locating specific information
- Guessing vocabulary in context

Assessment Link

- When was your first assessment completed to determine placement and performance of ELL studentss in general-education classes?
- What assessment type did you use? Did it contain all elements to assess struggling ELL students?
- Do all ELL students fit the definition of "struggling ELL students" as defined and adopted by teachers?
- How and when do you update assessments to determine students who are still struggling or at risk?

Many of their lower-performing ELL students need extra support and intervention so the co-teachers decide who is going to lead the lesson and who will support the ELL students' inaccurate miscues with decoding and multisyllabic words. Additionally, many ELL students have not yet developed the phonic and phonemic awareness to help understand the concepts of words, which interferes with fluency.

Because Ms. Grucelski has a good relationship with her co-teacher, they are both able to "play off" each other in the classroom. For example, she might "pretend" she doesn't understand something regarding types of rock erosions and ask the students before she asks her co-teacher in a fun and entertaining sort of way.

In another co-teaching scenario with a social studies teacher, Ms. Grucelski will ask the students if they can think of other topics that are similar to mollusks killing organisms. Students suggested the idea of the British colonizing the Americans, which reinforces cross-content teaching.

CRITICAL AREAS OF CO-TEACHING IN EARLY PRIMARY GRADES

The type of co-teaching and collaboration model greatly determines academic success. When ELL students lack background knowledge in a particular area of concept and important vocabulary, for example, teachers can use the turn-taking model where the content-area teacher provides content and the ESL teacher provides isolated linguistic support.

Elements of "quality instruction" (Calderon, 2011; August & Shanahan, 2006) particularly for first-graders of English learning, must include crucial instructional components of a comprehensive approach to teaching reading that includes phonemic awareness, decoding, vocabulary, reading comprehension, and writing. Opportunities for learning need to be extended to the end of the second grade to allow ELL students to catch up with their native English-speaking peers. The five co-teaching scenarios illustrated show how co-teachers can practice various problematic areas for struggling ELL students.

On the Level of Word Analysis

1. Both the ESL and General-Education Teacher Instruct in Front of the Class

The core teacher explicitly teaches the blending of individual sounds into words (this could also be in the areas of academic language of mathematics and science) to assist ELL students with the word-recognition process. The ESL teacher provides examples, clarifies, uses visuals, and restates using cognates and other targeted vocabulary. Teachers continue to provide more complex activities as students demonstrate more phonemic awareness and knowledge.

2. *Switching Roles 50 Percent of Class Time*

The core teacher instructs vowel-consonant and consonant-vowel word types to consonant blends, vowel digraphs, and letter-sound associations. The ESL teacher monitors and assesses.

Other areas of instruction include inflected endings and word roots to extend the students' word-recognition abilities.

On the Level of Reading Comprehension

1. Class Is Divided in Half and Both Teach the Same Content to a Heterogeneous Group

Both teachers are well-skilled in sheltering content to a specific content area. The core teacher develops listening comprehension to a read-aloud and models the use of how, what, when, and where questions to clarify information in the text or the meaning of words and sentences.

2. Turn-taking

ESL teacher pre-teaches vocabulary and reviews previously learned ideas and vocabulary relevant to the text. The core teacher presents the concepts. The ESL teacher asks/clarifies questions and elicits summaries from students by having them retell the central ideas of expository or narrative passages—this helps with the process of learning and expanding their knowledge of vocabulary and reinforces use of new vocabulary.

Vocabulary Instruction

1. Switching Roles 50 Percent of Class Time

The core teacher provides explicit vocabulary instruction on how to use context and surrounding text to understand the meaning of unknown words at the beginning of the lesson. The ESL teacher monitors or assesses students' comprehension of specific words and clusters in stories and/or nonfiction texts, and then they switch roles.

COLLABORATING ON TARGETED READING SKILLS AND STANDARDS

Teachers need to collaborate in areas of reading instruction to bring ELL students to state and national standards of learning including associations such as the National Association for Bilingual Education (NABE) and the National Council of Accreditation for Teacher Education (NCATE), TESOL, and the most recent initiative relating to CCSS. However, these standards do not provide the guidance as to how teachers can collaborate to help ELL students meet these standards.

Collaborating on benchmarks and educational standards common to all general content areas establishes what students should know and be able to do across content areas. For example, expecting ELL students to skim a paragraph to find the main idea may be a common educational standard across content areas, but in order for it to be *achievable*, it must also be *feasible*. This is where collaboration can be most useful in determining areas of reading and decoding that cause difficulty.

Once teachers know students' proficiency levels in reading, they can implement the acronym *SEAT* to collaborate on areas of instruction that specifically pertain to reading, as illustrated in table 3.1.

Best Practices in the Classroom: Co-creating a Language Objective in the Content Area of Math

The principal at the Partnership Academy expects teachers of ELL students to create a language objective for Math. As Kelly Grucelski and her co-teacher

Table 3.1. Collaborating on Standard-Driven Activities in Reading Comprehension

	S	E	A	T
	Area(s) of strength in decoding and early reading skills	Enabling benchmarks and skills needed for ELL students to succeed in content areas	Ways co-teachers can align core content objectives to provide more targeted areas of practice	Type of exercise* teachers can use to evaluate each objective
Corresponding Standards				

*Types of exercise can include multiple-choice items, matching items, open-ended questions, closes, true/false type questions.

model for their students, they ask themselves, *How can we be very clear in terms of our expectations?* This is where co-creating a language objective in Math, for example, can be particularly helpful.

Their objectives are to have their struggling ELL students write fractions and understand that they are a part of a whole. Students will be able to identify the numerator and denominator and say "one tenth" or "two eighths." They will also need to concentrate on making sure they say the right sound endings.

COLLABORATING IN THE MOST CRITICAL YEAR: FIRST GRADE

First-grader Miguel is a newcomer to an elementary school in a New York City public school district consisting of a large number of ELL students. He does not yet know the difference between letter sounds and letter names. His limited oral vocabulary and academic understanding and language of the content areas cause him to struggle in areas of reading and decoding.

Collaborating for the sake of the student like Miguel will lessen the academic and language gap between Miguel and average-achieving first-grade students. But the fact is first graders do not have plenty of time to improve and catch up with native English-speaking peers. Content and ESL teachers need to collaborate to provide core practices to general education students, but with added emphasis to provide second-language acquisition and support for ELL students. The evaluation checklist below focuses on areas of collaboration that are related to the areas of reading instruction.

Collaboration for each of the following areas in *reading instruction* can include any of the following area(s):

1. assessment;
2. model of collaboration;
3. individual student plan;
4. reading as a primary problem;
5. responsibility for struggling ELLs in ESL/general-education settings;
6. evaluation;
7. contact with parents and others;
8. record-keeping by ESL teachers;
9. student consent; parental objection.

THE COLLABORATIVE DYNAMICS BETWEEN AN ESL TEACHER AND READING TEACHER/SPECIALIST

One of the main issues that concern both ESL and reading teachers and specialists has to do with the role of reading comprehension and more specifically, how ELL students acquire these deeper comprehension skills.

The process by which an ELL student might be affected by the rate of acquiring comprehension skills depends on many variables including former schooling, learning styles, and motivation among many other subjects. To understand the factors that cause ELL students to acquire reading comprehension at a rate that is slower and results in a widening achievement gap, one needs to examine the role of second-language acquisition and its role in teaching a comprehensive approach to reading comprehension. Calderon (2011) states that reading comprehension correlates with content and procedural knowledge.

By understanding the process by which ELL students acquire the basic building blocks of early language and comprehension skills, co-teachers can enter the mind of a second-language learner. So much of what a teacher of ELL students does in the classroom is based on some kind of theory of language and how language is learned. For example, when a general-education teacher or reading teacher notices one of her ELL students encountering reading difficulties, she or he might ask herself, *How can this activity support the language-learning development of my ELL students?* Answering this question has practical and theoretical implications for second-language acquisition and reading comprehension as well.

In this respect, the ESL teacher can act as a language consultant to clarify second-language acquisition issues since she or he is equipped with a background in theory. As Brown (2005) states, "There are many competent ESL teachers whose expert knowledge can be of great assistance to general education teachers. Extending ESL teachers' role to include them as consultants to general education teachers is a way to address the current situation" (para. 6).

Specifically, an ESL teacher uses her expertise and knowledge of language-acquisition theory to complement the reading teacher's expertise of literacy so that, ultimately, both teachers coordinate quality instruction within and across grade levels and in co-teaching. The question that frequently arises among teachers is how to coordinate quality instruction within and across grade levels and in co-teaching.

The following set of questions should be kept handy to act as a check-up every six to eight weeks:

- To what degree did our collaboration help ELL students progress in both vocabulary and reading-proficiency levels?
- How did our collaboration help students make more connections with what they read?
- What theoretical model provides the most useful input for additional practice in reading comprehension?
- How can theories of second-language acquisition inform reading instruction?

A second-language teacher's instruction is based on some kind of theory of language and how language is learned. When it comes to providing culturally and linguistically responsive instruction, teachers should articulate reasons for their choices. ESL consultants who are language consultants, for example, can help general-education teachers with the process of identifying "a good theory," which, according to Professor Penny Ur (2001), "should generate an enormous amount of practice, by providing an idea which [teachers] can apply to lots of different classroom procedures" (1999).

Table 3.2 illustrates some of the ways an ESL teacher can enhance a dialogue with a reading teacher (and vice versa) in the areas of reading instruction and vocabulary acquisition.

WHAT DOES THE RESEARCH SAY ABOUT HOW SECOND-LANGUAGE LEARNERS ACQUIRE AND RETAIN NEW VOCABULARY?

One of the more fundamental yet overlooked aspects of explicit vocabulary instruction involves teaching a targeted word in its context. Beginning from kindergarten, English language learners need to master three thousand to five thousand words a year in a variety of contexts and across subject areas. Teachers need strategies to reinforce meaningful vocabulary learning and, specifically, academic language in a variety of contexts. Therefore, it makes sense for co-teachers to understand which types of contexts and learning activities help ELL students acquire new vocabulary words most effectively.

As described in the chart, Mondria (1993), for example, distinguished between types of contexts and types of learning activities to help teachers understand how to facilitate meaning. When ELL students lack knowledge in spelling, pronunciation, background knowledge, unfamiliar words, or false cognates, teachers can facilitate the learning and retention of new words before, during, and after reading. That way, they have a better chance

Table 3.2. Monitoring SLA Issues for ESL and Reading Teachers

Problematic Area of Reading	Relevant SLA Issues/Theories	Purpose/ Explanation of the SLA Issue/Theory	Practical Pedagogical Areas
Difficulties recognizing sounds/blends/ words in context and making connections in meaning	Awareness of interlanguage	Helps teachers anticipate certain difficulties ELL learners might encounter	Aids in appropriate error correction
Lack of progress in making deeper connections with reading comprehension	Formal content and linguistic schema Connection to the "silent period" of learning a second language		Observe/measure formal content and linguistic schema.
Challenges in recognizing and producing vocabulary	Supporting vocabulary/ language progression		
Retaining word meanings	Meaning inferred (Mondria, 1993) of vocabulary instruction	Words that occur in highly predictable contexts will probably be better retained than words that occur in nonpredictable contexts. Words learned with the help of texts are best retained.	When teaching new words, use them in a context of sentences or texts. For cost-efficient teaching, use the meaning-given method.

of reinforcing vocabulary knowledge with content knowledge and reading comprehension. Mondria (1993) discusses the types of effective contexts for teaching vocabulary:

- Effects of types of contexts
  - Words learned in sentences are better retained than words learned in isolation. Sentence context is helpful for learning words.

- Words learned with the help of texts are best retained. Texts offer better possibilities to keep students occupied for a longer period with word learning.
- Effects of types of learning activity
  - When words are learned with the help of a sentence context, the meaning-inferred method *is not better* than the meaning-given method.
- Effects of the factors "guessing-verifying-memorizing"
  - The act of only guessing leads to a small amount of retention.
  - Adding a verifying stage (e.g., let's check your responses) after guessing improves retention.
  - The memorizing stage is the most important part of the "meaning-inferred method," which is responsible for 66 percent of retention.

Understanding the role of background knowledge has important implications for collaboration on areas of reading comprehension as illustrated in the following section on schemata.

PUTTING THE SCHEMATA THEORY INTO COLLABORATIVE ACTION

The interplay between formal, content, and linguistic schemata and resulting impact on L2 reading is by far one of the most sweeping factors to consider when teaching second-language reading. Research into schema theory and its effects on L2 reading has been conducted since the 1970s (Aebersold & Field, 1997).

Schemata is an important influence on second-language reading skills, which is commonly referred to as *background* or *prior knowledge*. Gathering this information is both crucial and necessary when determining the kinds of reading tasks ELL students can and cannot do. There are various types of schema co-teachers can incorporate when discussing the difficulties of ELL students. Co-teachers can work from a much more informed place of planning when they know this information.

Content schema can be measured using pre-assessments to evaluate what ELL students already know about the target language in areas of vocabulary and reading comprehension. Linguistic schema, which relates to actual phonemic awareness in words, then placing words into phrases and finally into sentences, can also be measured using informal and formal assessments as well as from observing students.

Cognitive and affective domains in reading include specific things ELL students know about reading and how they feel about them. At the early elementary level, for example, teachers acquire important information about ELL students' attitudes toward reading, purposes for literacy, and their beliefs about reading, which are referred to as the cognitive and affective domains. These areas are represented by the questionnaire below, which co-teachers can use as a springboard into deciding which activities would be helpful to include particularly for their struggling ELL students.

Getting to Know the Reading Attitudes of Your ELL Students

1. What is their purpose for reading? (Is the purpose for pleasure or to respond to reading-comprehension questions?)
2. How do they feel about reading? (Do they like to choose books or like reading loudly to themselves or with a friend? Do they enjoy reading books in class? Do they enjoy listening to the teacher reading books aloud or participate when making predictions about a book?)
3. What are their past reading experiences? (Have they read an entire book? If so, what kinds—fiction or nonfiction? Are they able to access academic vocabulary for nonfiction texts?)
4. What do students do when they don't know a word? (Do they reread it, ask the teacher, or check the dictionary?)

As teachers learn more about their ELL students, they are more informed about the areas that cause ELL students to struggle and can consequently make better decisions about the academic needs of their ELL students in their co-teaching lessons. Activating background knowledge helps with the process of engaging ELL students deeper in the reading-comprehension process. Specifically, co-teachers can discuss possibilities on how to coordinate their roles especially when they are both providing direct instruction at the very beginning of a reading lesson.

THE ROLE OF BACKGROUND KNOWLEDGE IN COLLABORATION

Background knowledge is the experience and knowledge a student brings to classroom learning. When ELL students are just beginning to read, they need to know the words and concepts first. As Robert Marzano (2004) puts it, "Background knowledge is the interaction of students' information-processing abilities and their access to academically oriented experiences, then, that produces their academic background knowledge. Differences in these factors create differences in their academic background knowledge and, consequently, differences in their academic achievement" (para. 8).

This conscious and deliberate planning requires teachers to work "together in a supportive and mutually beneficial relationship; a style for direct interaction between at least two coequal partners voluntarily engaged in shared decision making as they work toward a common goal" (Friend & Cook, 1992).

In their discussions, for example, around background knowledge, teachers may ask, *How can we divide class time to provide extra linguistic support?* Or they may ask, *How can we differentiate instruction so all students can have full and equal access to academic content and reading comprehension?* Additionally, teams of bilingual/ESL and general-education teachers can also infuse multicultural concepts that help with the process of enhancing background knowledge into the general-education and content-area curriculum.

When ELL students are just beginning to make connections with academic content, they need to know the academic terminology and concepts first. In a co-teaching setting, an ESL teacher pre-teaches this content depending on the content-area vocabulary. That way, when the teacher shares an informational piece or walks ELL students through a problem, ELL students will have the background and vocabulary.

Professor Diane Barone encourages content-area teachers to spend at least seven to ten minutes pre-teaching academic vocabulary, which she refers to as "fancy words" (2008). Using English as the oral language of instruction requires agreeing on the various elements of how co-teachers will introduce and reinforce areas of academic language (i.e., text-based language) and the collaborative model that would best support oral instruction. In such a way, teachers emphasize successful oral practices and instructional strategies for ELL students who "do not get access to curriculum because they do not understand their teachers' instruction in general education classes" (Brown & Bentley, 2004).

As illustrated in the following three scenarios, each collaborative context presents possible configurations of how co-teachers can help ELL students acquire academic language content using oral instruction.

Additional suggested collaborative activities in the area of background knowledge can be seen in the following scenarios.

1. At the very beginning of the school year when they are just learning their ELL students' backgrounds and academic abilities, both ESL and general-education teachers begin sharing their observations and insights.
2. Using a turn-taking collaborative model, teachers take turns pre-teaching content. That way, when content-area or ESL teachers are sharing a story or informational piece, their ELL students will have the necessary background and vocabulary.

3. Teachers can share cultural information at regular faculty meetings for the purpose of clarifying students' behavior and sensitizing teachers to cultural differences. Content-area teachers can follow up with the ESL teachers on how to strengthen background knowledge and increase academic performance. Dual-language teachers will find it especially important to tap into the meaning of specific words in the subjects ELL students have to learn to access the meaning, context, and usage of words.

STRATEGIES FOR BUILDING BACKGROUND KNOWLEDGE

Even if ELL students have little or no content knowledge or confidence in their language ability and reading comprehension, teachers need to be able to elicit background knowledge. It is not that ELL students do not have background knowledge; they have it in another language. This implies that an ELL students' background knowledge is in the context of their culture, which may be very different than the culture of their classmates.

In this respect, teachers can build background knowledge physically, visually, and with sentence frames.

Physical and Visual Support

- **Co-teachers use concrete objects to introduce or reinforce a theme.** Examples: If the concept is baseball, bring in a baseball, a mitt, or a bat. If students are reading a text on tea, bring tea bags and let the students feel them and smell them up close as you read aloud from a story or reference text. It's a great way to add direct experience to the virtual experience of reading.
- **Use a guest speaker.** For example, if the next unit includes putting out fires, invite the local fire department to talk about their current job. For ELL students needing linguistic support, teachers can also ask students to translate what the speaker says into their own language if this is possible.
- **Use visually appealing texts.** Use picture books, even in the upper grades. They are an invaluable resource and this kind of visual tool is a great way to connect in a direct manner. Teachers who don't have access to picture books can use visually attractive magazine pictures instead.
- **Use stimulating visuals.** Besides finding individual pictures of items, teachers can use music and short videos from the Internet to create a virtual field trip of experience.

Sentence Frames

- Provide sentence frames to help ELL students become more comfortable when speaking with a partner. Use sentence frames or starters ELL students can complete before learning a new concept. The best sentence frames are those that they can personalize. For examples, have students complete the following:
    - Whenever I smell _____ I'm reminded of _____.
    - I think _____ is a hero, because _____.
- Create sentence frames with the word *because* to have ELL students explain connections between previous learning and the new topic. Example: I think our next topic will be _____ because our last lesson was _____.

When ELL students are encouraged to talk more in complete sentences, they will start writing more in complete sentences.

Best Practices in the Classroom: The Role of Materials to Enhance Background Knowledge

One of the more challenging areas is to find appropriate reading materials with the right balance of concise text, content, and visual layout and design. The brief vignette below illustrates this case in point.

Following the news release of Verla Kay's newest picture book, *Hornbook and Inkwells*, which focuses on early colonial history, a school librarian at Pulaski Elementary School in the Christina School district in Wilmington, Delaware, shared her experiences on the author's Facebook page of how both she and the ELL teacher tried to teach colonial history as part of the state standards to their fourth- and fifth-graders. She wrote:

> Because these ELL students had so little background in historical matters, they also could not picture what things were like back then. Using Verla Kay's picture book which has a minimum of text on each page and describes what is going on for each page, students were easily able to translate and explain using a document camera and the projector in the classroom to zoom in on some of the images.

Both co-teachers report that using this text made all the difference in anchoring content and ELL students were engaged and ready for the reading task!

The ESL teacher provides visual support of reading texts by:

- sketching the meaning of words and sentences;
- using gestures and having students act out the meaning of different sentences and paragraphs;

- pointing to illustrations or diagrams when reading a text to help explain the meaning of vocabulary words or sentences; and
- using graphic organizers to show relationships between ideas in the text.

The general-education/content teacher provides familiar reading texts to help ELL students focus specifically on the vocabulary and language structures they have identified in their language objectives.

CHAPTER SUMMARY

Collaboration that is specifically coordinated between ESL and reading teachers and specialists helps further ELL students' reading development to ensure their success across content areas. Understanding second-language acquisition theories can also influence the dialogues and conversations teachers have regarding ELL students' unique struggles with acquiring vocabulary and language.

SUGGESTED ACTIVITIES FOR FURTHER COLLABORATION

Discuss the implications of background knowledge for the academic achievement of ELL students in your school. What is needed to close these gaps? Is it cultural knowledge? Content knowledge? A combination of these? Something else? Find a teacher who has found a way to elicit students' background knowledge around similar content, themes, or vocabulary you are currently teaching. Try this particular strategy or adapt it using another. Discuss your findings. What works? What didn't? What's next?

REFERENCES

Aebersold, J., & Field, M. L. (1997). *From reading to reading teacher.* New York: Cambridge University Press.

August, D., & Shanahan, T. (Eds.) (2006). Executive summary. *Developing literacy in second-language learners: Report of the National Literacy Panel on Language-Minority Children and Youth.* Mahwah, NJ: Lawrence Erlbaum Associates. Retrieved June 26, 2013, from www.cal.org/projects/archive/nlpreports/Executive_Summary.pdf

Barone, D. (2008). Interview. Someone I'd Like You to Meet: Professor Diane M. Barone. *New Teacher Resource Center.* http://newteacherresourcecenter.com/?p=537

Brown, C. L. (2005). Ways to help ELLs: ESL teachers as consultants. *Academic Exchange Quarterly, 9*(4).

Brown, C. L., & Bentley, M. (2004). ELLs: Children left behind in science class. *Academic Exchange Quarterly, 8*(3), 152–157.

Calderon, M. (2011). *Teaching reading to English language learners in K–5th grades*. Online course, Solution Tree Press.

Friend, M., & Cook, L. (1992). *Interactions: Collaboration skills for school professionals*. White Plains, NY: Longman.

Marzano, R. J. (2004). *Building background knowledge for academic achievement: Research on what works in schools*. Alexandria, VA: Association for Supervision and Curriculum Development.

Mondria, J-A. (1993). *The effects of different types of context and different types of learning activity on the retention of foreign language words.* Paper presented at the 10th AILA World Congress of Applied Linguistics, Amsterdam.

Snow, C. E., Burns, M. S., & Griffin, P. (1998). *Preventing reading difficulties in young children*. Washington, DC: National Academy Press.

Ur, Penny. (2001). There is nothing so practical as a good theory. *Pan Asia Consortium Journal, 1*, 33–40.

Chapter Four

Collaboration in the Development of Read-alouds, Academic Vocabulary, and Differentiated Instruction

When ELL students do not have access to enough academic vocabulary and content knowledge, they struggle with understanding academic texts. This situation creates even more challenges for teachers who already differentiate and target academic language for each proficiency level and range of schooling background. It is also not effective for the ESL teacher to teach all the required content words and vocabulary ELL students need for academic success. With effective planning and team teaching, however, both content and ESL teachers can support ELL students' progress through the different proficiency levels.

This chapter begins by providing information on using read-alouds with ELL students and explores a number of effective and practical ways to co-teach using read-alouds and the vocabulary of content areas and general collaborative planning strategies. Next, it explores various ways to teach academic vocabulary using the tier approach. It also considers some characteristics of how co-teachers can monitor areas of quality reading instruction and how ELL students acquire comprehension skills.

QUESTIONS

- How can teachers successfully use collaborative practices to enhance differentiated instruction for ELL students?
- What are some collaborative techniques and strategies that support ELL students in the early stages of learning to read?
- What are some of the ways co-teachers can provide vocabulary support in the four core subjects—math, science, social studies, and language arts and across the different proficiency levels?

TECHNIQUES FOR COLLABORATING ON THE STAGES OF A READ-ALOUD

A read-aloud is one way for teachers to balance literacy instruction, content, and skills. Research has established that effective read-alouds contribute to students' comprehension development (Fisher, Flood, Lapp, & Frey, 2004) and background knowledge, language, and listening comprehension skills (Beck & McKeown, 2001). To date, limited resources are available on co-teaching practices for the sake of using a balanced literacy framework in ESL and general-education classrooms.

However, much has been written on the benefits of using a balanced literacy approach. For ELL students who are not making incremental progress in early reading skills, a balanced reading approach is most effective for bridging word-text skills (August & Shanahan, 2006).

A balanced literacy approach gives many opportunities for teachers to co-plan a wide variety of skills using a three-stage approach. The "while or during reading" stage, for example, is particularly important for bridging word-text-based skills. In this way, teaching a read-aloud would need to be broken down into smaller or different components.

Friend and Cook (2004) encourage teachers to consider "the content to be taught and the instructional strategies that are most effective for addressing the content. Highly structured content and procedures, such as teaching steps in a process, would require one approach while less structured content, such as a discussion of ideas, would suggest another approach." Therefore, when planning co-teaching lessons around a read-aloud, it is recommended to target a few content and linguistic areas for each of the three stages and to allow sufficient time and preparation for planning and teaching.

The initial planning resource illustrated in textbox 4.1 describes the various considerations ESL and content and/or reading teachers should use when targeting areas of a read-aloud.

The following resource details what specifically should happen during each of the three stages of a read-aloud lesson—the beginning (pre), the middle (during reading), and post (after) stages. Co-teachers can use the following suggestions below.

Before Read-aloud

- Model and build reading strategies using background knowledge.
- Brainstorm the cover of the book including the type of story. Teachers say and write the title on the board and encourage guessing while pointing out sound blends, letters, sounds, and patterns. Teachers can also point out that

TEXTBOX 4.1.
Criteria for Co-planning a Balanced Read-aloud Lesson

1. Transitions between activities
2. Targeted skill(s) for each of the three stages:

    Pre: _____

    During: _____

    After: _____
3. Procedures
4. Activities that help ELL students demonstrate their knowledge
5. Assessments
6. Types of available co-teaching models:

Selection:
- We chose this co-teaching model because _____
- We feel it would support our ELL students' _____
  because _____
  _____

- In order to minimize problems, we would need to do the following:
  1. _____
  2. _____
  3. _____

the illustrator and the author could be the same person, as well as point out the dedication, publisher, and other bibliographic information.
- Teachers flip through the books and have students answer the following questions:
  - Are there are a lot of pictures? What kinds (photos, drawings, cartoon strips)?
  - When does the story take place (a long time ago, now, in the future)? How do you know?
  - What do you think happens in the story?

- Do you think the story will be funny, exciting, boring, or interesting? How do you know?
- Do you think the story will be easy, just right, or difficult to understand? How do you know? (Adapted from *The Longman Guide to Graded Reading*, ed. by Livingstone et al., 1987.)
• Pre-teach vocabulary.

Read-alouds provide excellent opportunities for instructing and reinforcing new vocabulary in context. "Vocabulary development is a critical element of an effective English immersion program where reading instruction occurs in English simultaneously with English language development. Thus, vocabulary development must be integrated with all aspects of an [oral] instructional program" (Haager & Windmueller, 2001).

COLLABORATING ON PRESENTATION: ACCURACY AND MEANING

Pre-teaching vocabulary techniques should include elements of the word form as well as meaning, which are both necessary for later practice stages. The form of the vocabulary word should be practiced and presented in decoding- and phonic-based lessons where the teaching emphasis is primarily on accuracy. For the sake of collaboration, both teachers can take turns focusing on either accuracy or meaning-based elements of the targeted words. The read-look-say method, as illustrated below, is effective for helping students learn early decoding and reading skills according to word patterns. "[ELLs] need many opportunities to practice using language to organize their ideas and to remember" (Roskos, Tabors, & Lenhart, 2004). Additionally, teachers can anchor in the lexical item by using a contextual clue, a picture, or a string of associations that are presented orally and then written on the board so students can connect their associations to print.

Look-Read-Say Reading Technique

1. Teacher presents the word *ride* in a sentence strip in a variety of contexts (i.e., *ride* as a verb and a noun) and, finally, in question format: *Do you ride a bicycle after school, or do you go on a train ride to school?*
   a. Teacher says, "The word *ride* sounds like the word *side*."
   b. Students hear the pattern.
   c. Students say the word and spell out the word.

2. For a phonetic approach, teachers show a flashcard with a highlighted sound cluster. Students then say the name of the sound, then the sound within a word.
3. Self-check and practice:
   a. Students look at the word.
   b. Students say the word.
   c. Students cover the word.
   d. Students spell and write the word.
   e. Students check their work.

To ensure ELL students understand 99 percent of a spoken text, teachers need to provide opportunities to discuss vocabulary in context; otherwise ELL students may spend an inordinate amount of their cognitive energies trying to guess at the word's meaning, thus losing the flow of the story. According to Elisheva Barkon (in Sasson, 2007), "In the early stages of teaching foreign language and second language reading, learners are learning to read not reading to learn. In other words, they are learning how to identify words automatically, accurately and rapidly. To that end, they need practice with easy texts where all the words are familiar so that they can develop sight vocabulary" (para. 4).

Before teachers focus on new vocabulary words, they may need to check students' familiarity with the context. On the tier 1 level, the word *gloves* in *Bear Snores On*, for example, is a basic word ELL students need to communicate, read, and write and one that needs to be explicitly taught. The word *gloves* should be associated with *cold* and *hands*. Teachers will want to teach new vocabulary, such as the word *gloves*, in the context by providing oral contextual clues to help students recognize the meaning either independently or with the teacher's help. The focus of such vocabulary instruction is on the context to aid in teaching and reinforcing the meanings of new words. Examples of discussing the target vocabulary in relation to the read-aloud theme might include discussing the word *snores*. *What does the bear do when he is sleeping*? Other collaboration methods for using oral instruction to support reading instruction and academic vocabulary can be found in table 4.1.

Nonverbal (i.e., gestures) and verbal clue (i.e., pictures) facilitate the process of scaffolding between hearing words and seeing them in their respective contexts before students have the necessary reading skills to acquire vocabulary independently.

The stages for discussing new vocabulary should follow several teaching principles relating to a particular pattern of development.

Table 4.1. Collaborating on Oral Instructional Goals

ESL Oral Instructional Goals	Oral Instructional Goals in a General-Education Class	Suggested Activities to Develop Fluency in Oral Work	Content Objectives
Articulate sounds, whole words, or sentences in a creative way	Practice articulating dialogues, stories, texts	Role play (verbal) Choral and echo reading Sing, chant, recite, or rhyme a poem or a song on a cassette	Fluency, vocabulary work
Use greetings, farewells in short exchanges	Use greetings, farewells in longer exchanges	Conversation in pairs	Fluency, vocabulary work, comprehension
Engage in a simple conversation on a familiar topic	Engage in simple conversation on a less familiar topic	Conversation in pairs	Fluency, vocabulary, comprehension
Understand spoken message (with help of pictures)	Understand spoken message (with help of pictures)	Students fill in a report based on listening to specific information or draw pictures based on a listening task (e.g., color the clown)	Vocabulary, comprehension
Understand simple instructions	Understand more complex instructions	Put pictures in the right order, describe a picture	Vocabulary, fluency, comprehension
Present simple information—use words learned in an authentic context	Present more complex information—use words learned in an authentic context	Students make a project: me, my family, my pet, my room, etc. (pictures or models with word labels)	Fluency, vocabulary, comprehension
Teach reading	Teach reading	Present and reinforce whole words	Vocabulary, comprehension

ESL Oral Instructional Goals	Oral Instructional Goals in a General-Education Class	Suggested Activities to Develop Fluency in Oral Work	Content Objectives
Production of texts on a word or sentence level via pre/during/post activities: • prediction • finding main idea • brainstorming • sequencing • matching pieces of information • vocabulary work	Production of texts on a word or sentence level via pre/during/post activities: • prediction • finding main idea • brainstorming • sequencing • matching pieces of information • vocabulary work • fluency—timed readings	Read-alouds: students complete tasks based on a narrative or expository text	Vocabulary, comprehension

During the Read-aloud

Teachers start reading the book to the class and, while reading, they can do one or more of the following activities.

1. Work with Plot and Characters

While reading activities provide opportunities for co-teachers to review the story's plot and characters. In the case of collaboration, the reading teacher can pre-teach the concept of a "story map" while the ESL teacher elicits from students evidence or interpretation of specific details from the text to general assumptions about the characters.

2. Elicit Predictions from Students about What Could Occur Next

(In dual-language classrooms, ELL students' responses can be written in their mother tongue.) Teachers can also facilitate discussions around relevant concepts to the story. The reading teacher stops the read-aloud at a particular place and facilitates the discussion of students' predictions in the area of content (e.g., plots, characters, and story sequence) while the ESL teacher confirms predictions of specific and relevant vocabulary.

Prediction is another way to encourage students to think about possibilities in a text. Using the very popular read-aloud *Bear Snores On* by Karma Wilson (2003), both the ESL and reading teacher facilitate comprehension and concept understanding of cause-effect integral to the story. For example, one possibility for collaboration is for either the ESL or reading teacher to pre-teach the concepts of *cause* and *effect* by introducing it authentically.

Example of a Script

When your mother tries to wake you up in the morning to get up for school, she is trying to cause *you to wake up. Something happens in our story to* cause *bear to finally stop his snoring. Do you remember what it is?*
While reading question:
Let's read it again together and see if we can pick out the word (or words) that causes bear to suddenly wake up.
Hare stokes the fire.
Mouse seasons stew.
Then a small pepper fleck
Makes the bear . . . RAAAAA-CHOOOOOO!

Implications for Collaboration

As the ESL teacher reads, the reading teacher can ask the "during reading" question and show students pictures in preparation for discussing the concept of *effect*.

- *What does this noise* cause *all the animals to do?* Students look at the pictures. (Possible answers: They hide from the noise; they run away; they cover their heads and ears.)
- The reading teacher can also discuss the term *effect*. What *effect* do the animals' reactions have in the story? If bear's sneeze *causes* the animals to hide from the noise or run away, what is the *effect, or what happens,* because of those actions?
- *Now, back to you. When you first wake up, are you grouchy? Let's take a look at bear here. Does he look happy to you? What does he do?* Teacher reads the part about the bear's reaction ("And the bear wakes up! Bear gnarls and he snarls. Bear roars and he rumbles! Bear jumps and he stomps. Bear growls and he grumbles.") Teacher draws attention to the fact that these are, in fact, rhyming words. (See appendix for additional student and teacher pages for *Bear Snores On*.)

AFTER READ-ALOUDS

Think-alouds

According to Tomlinson and Cooper (2006), think-alouds represent "a reading strategy in which a teacher or a student who is proficient with reading reads a key passage of material aloud and simultaneously explains their thinking about what they are reading. The procedure is a way of modeling for students how a good reader interacts with text to make meaning of it" (p. 45). Think-alouds also generate a personal response or cause students to think further about the story and its elements, which is an important reflection technique. Both ESL and reading teachers can stimulate their students' reaction to the material by using direct questioning to generate open responses, as illustrated in the following examples:

1. How would you feel if _____?
2. What would you do or say if _____?

Implications for Collaboration

The ESL teacher can model a wide array of responses while the reading teacher helps individual students. Group or pair work can also be used depending on how much both co-teachers wish to structure the activity.

In the following post-reading activity, both co-teachers work with individual groups or pairs modeling the activity while supporting students' writing and speaking.

Summary Writing

Summarizing is one of the hardest skills to teach. Co-teachers can facilitate this process and help ELL students summarize either the entire read-aloud or part of the read-aloud by breaking down the different parts.

1. Have students summarize the story, showing its structure clearly.
2. Using the direct instruction of a turn-taking model, the ESL teacher pre-teaches the structure of summary writing. He or she provides sentence starters to help students create a new oral text that represents the read-aloud they have just heard while clarifying the concept of the activity and vocabulary.

Examples:

- This story tells about a _____.
- This part is about the _____.
- One important fact here is that _____.

The reading teacher, on the other hand, can model how to tell the most important idea in a section of text, and distinguishing it from details that tell more about it. He or she elicits the various details using *WH* question words to anchor what students already know: Who? What? When? Where? How? Why? How much? and so on.

Examples:

- The main idea is _____.
- The key details that support that part of story are _____.
- The purpose of this story is to _____.

(Adapted from Calderon, 2011)

PARTNER READING

Another way to gauge ELL students' comprehension of a read-aloud is through partner reading. Either using direct instruction or switching roles, co-teachers can model comprehension strategies before expecting their students to summarize orally what they have read. Both of the following co-teaching scenarios support this modeling of instruction.

Scenario #1: Direct instruction—before expecting ELL students to engage in after partner reading, the core teacher teaches content using reading and modeling strategies. The ESL teacher provides examples, clarifies, uses visuals, and restates.

Scenario #2: Switching roles 50 percent of class time, where the core teacher teaches and the ESL teacher monitors or assesses students, and then they switch roles. Therefore, in a forty-five-minute lesson, ideally the ESL teacher will monitor how well ELL students are engaged in this activity for twenty minutes after the core teacher models instruction before progressing to the next sequence.

Between themselves, co-teachers can model the procedure of "partner reading" (see next page) before expecting students to do this on their own.

Alternatively, the ESL teacher can work with a small group of ELL students in a corner.

Procedure: Partner Reading

- *Sequence #1: "Pure reading"*
  - Partner A reads the first sentence. Partner B helps.
  - Partner B reads the next sentence. Partner A helps.
- *Sequence #2: "Summarization"*
  - After each paragraph, partners "put their heads together" and summarize what they read.
  - Partners continue until they finish reading the assigned section.

At various intervals, both teachers can stop the lesson and model some "troubleshooting" tactics that may arise during the lesson. By doing so, teachers can bring in more strategy-building (activity adapted from Calderon, 2011).

A list of additional post-reading activities can be found below.

TEXTBOX 4.2.
Ten Post-reading Activities

1. Compare and contrast the read-aloud with another book students have read: plots, characters, theme, style, etc.
2. Have students choose a character they particularly liked—or disliked—and say why they liked/disliked him/her.
3. Have students write a poem about the story, or about one character or event or place in it.
4. Have students identify and discuss the main conflicts in the story. How are they resolved?
5. Have students answer the question: Did anything in the read-aloud disappoint you? What, and why?
6. Have students change the setting of the story (time or place). How does it affect the story?
7. Have students tell the story from the point of view of one of the characters.
8. Have students write a letter to the author of the book and explain the effect the book had on them.
9. Have students write a diary for one of the characters about his/her situation.
10. Have students write a letter to one of the characters, expressing their opinions about his/her situation and behavior.

COLLABORATING ON A READ-ALOUD: PUTTING IT ALL TOGETHER

To use read-alouds successfully to help develop literacy skills, teachers need to consider the place read-alouds have in the overall classroom environment and instruction. They will want to consider specific instructional goals and evaluation of student progress in achieving those goals. The next three textboxes (4.3, 4.4, and 4.5) include a checklist, a planning template, and lesson organizer, respectively, designed to aid teachers in thinking through the considerations when structuring successful read-aloud experiences for their students.

TEXTBOX 4.3.
Checklist: Collaborating on a Read-aloud: Putting It All Together

Co-Teacher's Checklist
My role: _____
I complement my co-teacher in the following areas:
_____

Structure

- What is the role of the read-aloud in our current reading program (e.g., reading for pleasure, vocabulary, comprehension, information about text)?
- What are some of the intended skills (e.g., vocabulary, comprehension, literal and inferential comprehension)?

Time Management

- How much time will we devote to read-alouds weekly?
- How will we structure our read-aloud sessions (e.g., within a general reading lesson, as part of an independent reading session)?

Maintenance and Follow-up

- How will we document and monitor progress?
- What benchmarks will we use?
- How will we ensure the integrity of our methodology regarding read-alouds?

Appropriation of Roles
In a read-aloud, who does what?

- Explicit vocabulary instruction and direct modeling
- Providing direct comprehension strategies
- Reading the story aloud
- Activating background knowledge
- Discussing and explaining vocabulary in context
- Providing direct instruction (e.g., information on instructions, procedures for activities, clarifying and discussing new approaches)

When using oral instruction, what is the purpose?

- To frame the context for "teacher academic talk"
- To teach new information
- To teach a new procedure
- To help students facilitate the process of understanding new information
- To help students organize their materials before, during, and after an oral/reading activity.
- What collaborative method will be used?
- What is the instructional setting? Whole-class or small-group framework?

> **TEXTBOX 4.4.**
> **Collaborative Lesson Organizer**
>
> **The Pre-lesson**
> *Who will do what? (See appendix for chart outlining issues to be decided between general education teachers and ESL teachers)*
>
> Name of co-teacher and specific activities:
>
> Name of teacher and specific activities:
>
> Purpose of each activity (e.g., activating background knowledge, anticipating the story's contents):
>
> 1. _____
> 2. _____
>
> Transition links:
>
> **The Middle**
> Name of teacher and specific activities:
>
> Name of teacher and specific activities:
>
> Purpose of each activity (e.g., confirming predictions, discussing concepts):
>
> 1. _____
> 2. _____
>
> Transition links:
>
> **The End of the Lesson**
> Name of teacher and specific activities:
>
> Name of teacher and specific activities:
>
> Purpose of each activity (e.g., to summarize the story, expand on the story's theme):
>
> 1. _____
> 2. _____

Evaluating Students
Reflection—After the Lesson:
What has changed in students' learning as a result of using this particular collaborative model? How did students respond to this new collaborative model? How did it further our instructional goals? What implications does this have for further collaboration?

TEXTBOX 4.5.
Planning Template: Implementing a Collaborative Model in Reading

Use this template at the onset of implementing a collaborative model for the first time or if changing to a different model.

Names of teachers:

Class/grade(s):

Lesson(s):

Targeted skill(s) and objective(s):

Other skills ELL students might need:

Date and time:

Type of model:

- Educational advantages from using this model:

- Time management benefits from using this model (How will our collaboration be maximized?):

- Instructional benefits from using this model:

Materials and other resources needed:

EXPLICIT VOCABULARY INSTRUCTION IN COLLABORATIVE ACTION (READ-ALOUDS)

In the read-aloud *Bear Snores On* (Wilson, 2003) the ESL teacher teaches the word *gloves* in the context by providing oral contextual clues to help students recognize the meaning either independently or with the teacher's help. (Teachers may need to check students' familiarity with the context.) When teachers focus on the context, they are able to reinforce the meanings of new words. Examples of discussing the target vocabulary in relation to the read-aloud theme might include:

- Teacher discusses the word "grouchy" as the underlying theme for Eric Carle's *The Grouchy Ladybug* using a picture of a grouchy face.
- Teacher explicates the word "snores" in *Bear Snores On*. *What does the bear do when he is sleeping?*

Non-verbal (i.e., gestures) and verbal clues (i.e., pictures) facilitate the process of scaffolding between hearing words and seeing them in their respective contexts before students have the necessary reading skills to acquire vocabulary independently.

In a read-aloud context, teachers should ideally provide a range of language scaffolds so all ELL students can map out the basic story components of plot and character and understand basic vocabulary integral to the read-aloud.

Language scaffolds that can be used in any collaborative setting include:

- using simple and concrete language to introduce and discuss new vocabulary;
- using modeling strategies to help facilitate comprehension;
- anticipating and predicting further content;
- encouraging ELL students to make connections with what they have heard; and
- pre-teaching vocabulary before reading a story.

COLLABORATING ON EXPLICIT VOCABULARY INSTRUCTION

Numerous researchers have identified vocabulary in kindergarten and first grade as a significant predictor of reading comprehension in the middle and secondary grades (Cunningham & Stanovich, 1997) or reading difficulties (Chall & Dale, 1995; Denton & Hocker, 2006). Teachers of ELL students can provide multiple opportunities to integrate explicit vocabulary instruction in a reading lesson. At the K–1 grade level, general-education teachers and ESL teachers can collaborate on the following:

1. selecting and choosing appropriate content words to pre-teach (see appendix for chart outlining issues to be decided between general education teachers and ESL teachers)
2. appropriate roles before, during, and after reading;
3. deciding on the reading/speaking context for exposure and practice of new words and text-based skills; and
4. deciding on various co-teaching and other collaborative contexts that are best suited for explicit vocabulary instruction.

Sample scenario: pre-teaching and reinforcing the vocabulary word *manage* using a fifth-grade text. Note how the examples below support progress both in four language domains and in different contexts including a core subject area.

1. Teacher says the word: "Say *manage* three times."
2. Teacher states the word in context from the text of other content areas: "Although many species *manage* to survive such extreme...."
3. Teacher provides the dictionary definition(s): (1) succeed in doing something difficult; (2) to be in charge of, to run: *manage* a company.
4. Teacher explains the meaning with student-friendly definitions: "I *managed* to lose ten pounds by exercising. My father *manages* that store."
5. Teacher highlights features of the word: polysemous, cognate, tense, prefixes, etc. "*Manage* is a polysemous word. *Manejar* is the cognate. It also has multiple meanings (to drive, to manage)."
6. Teacher engages students in activities to develop word/concept knowledge. *Think-pair-share*: "What have you *managed* well recently?"
7. Teacher engages students in activities to develop word/concept knowledge: "Remember to use *manage* in your summaries." (Taken from Calderon, 2011)

MAKING READING CONNECTIONS

The acronym *PRO* illustrates the connection between understanding academic content and the meaning of academic words across subject areas.

1. **Purpose:** What is the purpose of using this academic word? How will it help ELL students understand the content of the passage?

2. **Reading concept:** What is the purpose of using this activity in this particular narrative or expository text? How does it help target necessary benchmarks and skills?
3. **Orientation:** What will teachers need to do to orient ELL students to the language, content, and structure of the read-aloud?

Best Practices in the Classroom

At the Rocky Point School district, Nicole Fernandez works in a push-in setting and collaborates with both a content-area teacher and a reading specialist to create a more balanced literacy program with the emphasis on read-alouds. She states, "I have been teaching for the last six years as a pull out teacher and found that the students were so detached from their classroom and struggling academically and socially. This past year, we put all twelve ESL children in a second-grade classroom. Those students consist of beginner, intermediate, advanced, and transitional students along with the majority native English speakers. This method allows me to co-teach in the classroom between three to four periods. I am there to help modify and enhance instruction for writing, math, and reading groups (centers). Academically, they are still below but have made much more gains in the classroom."

Each content area has its own balanced literacy theme unit that includes language, content, and literacy components. For example, a balanced theme social studies unit in her second-grade ESL classroom can look like this:

> **Subject:** Social Studies
> **Unit:** Map/Camping
> **Time period:** three weeks
> **TPR:** To teach children cardinal directionals and maps. The lesson would begin with directions around the room where children would walk around and give each other directions using cardinal directions.
> **PowerPoint:** A PowerPoint presentation would follow introducing new vocabulary and discussing where they have heard words such as *lantern, hiking, tent,* etc. Students discuss new words that will be heard in the story accompanied by a picture. New words are put in a sentence to ensure understanding.
> **Writing:** Students will write spooky stories about a pretend or real camping trip that will be shared at the end of the unit around a pretend campfire. Students eat marshmallows while reading stories. In general, students write a story once a week based on the topic being covered in class.
> **Reading:** Review vocabulary and read a story from the anthology *Starry Skies*. The story will be read aloud and critical thinking questions will be asked. Guided-reading books are selected around the theme for that month as well as the writing topic.

Centers: Guided reading books—students will read books on their reading level about camping. Comprehension questions will be asked and they will practice writing questions in complete answers.

Social Studies: Students will practice reading maps and then make their own maps of the school and their neighborhood using a technology program called "Neighborhood Map Machine."

THE BENEFITS OF THE PUSH-IN CONFIGURATION

Although it has been a challenge for administration to see the positive effects of this program in Ms. Fernandez's class, the students have enjoyed the program immensely. The ESL students have said that "they like it so much better because they are not lost in class anymore" and the general-education students are much more culturally aware and have gained new relationships. Nicole states that, academically, ELL students are still below but have made much more gains in the classroom. The parents of both mainstream students and ELLs are happy because there are two teachers in the room.

In Nicole Fernandez's words, "I believe if this program could start in kindergarten and follow them throughout the years they would not be so low. This is true collaboration because we both teach at the same time throughout the year and we modify as we need and work in groups as needed. This is the movement that needs to happen in order to decrease the gap of English Language Learners with their mainstream peers!"

Best Practices in the Classroom: Using Email as Follow-up

Collaborating on goals and activities is often a process of trial and error. This process requires extra coordination in a co-teaching situation when ELL students are learning a new concept or skill. In an email exchange, two co-teachers report difficulty with adding, but with the added communication they were able to reflect on the previous day's lessons and strategize the next day's lesson, and what she could do to help her ELL students progress in the areas of manipulatives in Math and phonics for reading. The following interaction can be seen in the below email exchange:

Day 1

Dyoungs: Next week, we will be starting two-digit addition.

Nfernandez: Thanks for letting me know. I will bring the manipulatives—tens blocks—and we will start with having them make tens blocks on day one and go from there.

Day 2

Dyoungs: The girls had a hard time with the adding. What do you want to do for tomorrow?

Nfernandez: Tomorrow I will pull the girls and two others that had a hard time during centers. I will re-teach and then preview the next day's lesson. Let's see if that helps. You can do reading groups and I will review.

Day 3

Nfernandez: The girls got the lesson yesterday. Today I will go back to reading groups and go over the long vowel sounds. Let me know how they do with homework tonight. I can always call them in for extra help this week if they are still having a hard time!

SUPPORTING ELL STUDENTS USING AN ACADEMIC VOCABULARY TIER FRAMEWORK OF INSTRUCTION

When collaborating in areas of academic language with other content-area teachers, it is helpful for teachers to view academic language based on the principles of "tiering" (Calderon, 2011). Since each tier targets vocabulary progress in reading and core subjects, teachers will need to take into account how each tier also affects their co-teaching and planning. In mixed-ability classes, teachers, for example, will need to differentiate academic language by targeting each proficiency level.

Academic Support for Tiers 1, 2, and 3

Vocabulary tier 1 includes basic words ELL students need to communicate, read, and write. These are simple words for English speakers, but might create difficulty for ELL students due to spelling, pronunciation, background knowledge, false cognates, and unfamiliar words, and need to be pre-taught, and key concepts need to be reviewed.

Vocabulary tier 2: Calderon refers to this group of words as "information processing words that nest tier 3 words in long sentences" (2011). In addition, teachers will need to teach cognates, polysemous words, transition words and connectors, phrasal clusters and idiomatic expressions, and rich language to indicate a number of similar expressions for discussions and descriptions. For example, if teachers have already taught the meanings of *talk* and *say* at the tier 1 level, they will need to teach other words such as *whisper, argue, specify, announce, request, reveal, remark, declare, describe, discuss, proclaim, shout,* and *scream*.

Vocabulary tier 3 includes subject-specific words that label content-discipline concepts, subjects, and topics as well as infrequently used academic words.

Academic Language Differentiation in Action Using Tier 3 Academic Content-Specific Words in Science

One way to differentiate and target academic language for each proficiency level is by grouping ELL students according to low-, middle-, and high-performing areas of reading and vocabulary instruction. By providing challenging and not-too-difficult reading texts and questions and vocabulary activities, each group of ELL students can progress according to their ability and pace, as illustrated in textbox 4.6.

Content-Area Targeted Science Vocabulary: Photosynthesis, Germ, Atom, Matter, Osmosis, Power

- *Lower-performing ELL students:* This group reads orally a list of targeted vocabulary words of varying length and difficulty, depending on their performance.
- *Middle-performing ELL students:* This group reads orally a list of targeted vocabulary words/sentences of varying length and difficulty and then matches the word to the picture or matches the sentence that describes the picture.
- *Higher-performing ELL students:* This group reads a short text of varying length and difficulty using the targeted words the teacher has taught previously. In pairs, they then read the sentence found in the text that corresponds to the questions. This assumes that ELL students have acquired a deeper meaning of the words and sentences.

Depending on the collaborative model and the students' proficiency levels, teachers can decide how to coordinate their own efforts to help them manipulate the level of the text. The information in textbox 4.7 guide teachers in coordinating fluency-building strategies and simplifying academic texts.

Best Practices in the Classroom

At the Sachem Central School District in New York, ESL teacher Aristea Lucas created and utilized collaborative sheets illustrated by textboxes 4.8 and 4.9 for content-area teachers when she taught at the K–5 level, and then incorporated them at the middle school level when she saw the need for it also

TEXTBOX 4.6.
Differentiating Academic Language at Various Reading Levels

1. Assign an easy reading task when a text is difficult and a challenging task when a text is easy. This "rule of thumb" is a practical way of creating lessons without having to rewrite texts on different levels to meet the needs of heterogeneous classes.
2. Use whole groups for modeling a concept and small groups for guided practice. Teachers can plan differentiated lessons more successfully by extending the main objective from whole group to small, differentiated groups during reading instruction.
3. Adapt reading activities to two or three different levels. Allow the student to choose the level where she or he can function.
4. Give open-ended exercises that allow students to work at their own pace and provide a variety of responses. Include tasks like brainstorming, prediction, and completing sentences.
5. Use different learning configurations such as group or pair work to appeal to mixed-ability classes. ELL students have a better chance of functioning better when they are paired with another student whose knowledge of English is not limited and/or who can speak the ELL student's mother tongue.
6. Provide ELL students with opportunities to work individually that allow them to progress at their own pace. In a regular day-to-day lesson, teachers can say, "Do as much of question 5 as you can in 10 minutes" or "Choose which question you want to start with."
7. Help English language learners master the spelling and the vocabulary of different lexical items by grouping words according to their learning abilities (i.e., lower-, middle-, and higher-performing groups). Teachers might also give ELL students two lists of words: one required and one optional.
8. Consider the needs of primary school children when planning differentiated lessons. Use small groups for short, focused instruction when there is a small group of students who struggle with an alphabet letter or sound.
9. Group children based on a book choice that supports a theme. If the theme is survival, for instance, each group of students would read a different book that shares this theme.

TEXTBOX 4.7.
Coordinating Content in Collaboration: Fluency-Building Strategies to Help with Simplifying Academic Texts

Name of text:_____

Content area(s) of instruction:_____

- Is the text on a motivating topic that relates to students' background knowledge?
- Did we provide sufficient vocabulary preparation prior to working on the text?
- Did we write difficult sentences to make them less ambiguous?
- Did we accompany texts with glossed words in an easy-to-understand context?
- Did we simplify language structure, syntax, and semantics?
- Did we link reading tasks with at least one oral activity such as echo or repeated reading?
- Did we identify different reading strategies for different texts?

Fluency-Building Tips

- Have beginning or struggling ELL students read words in meaningful contexts rather than focusing on word lists.
- Use sound spelling correspondences or "chunks" of words to help students read unfamiliar words.
- Use words that are a part of a student's oral vocabulary and that are more easily recognized and understood.
- Use texts where ELL students can identify 99 percent of the vocabulary. This also includes sight words. When used to support fluency, the right text can facilitate vocabulary learning and comprehension. To build oral fluency, use shorter texts with known vocabulary to consolidate practice and exposure.
- Teach visually appealing texts. Layout, print, type, and size all affect readability and motivation. A shorter text, for example, increases students' focus.
- Have students regulate themselves in terms of rate and prosody depending on the type of text or vocabulary.

TEXTBOX 4.8.

Collaborative Planning Sheet

ESL—Content-Area Support

Student _____

For the week of _____

Spelling: _____

Math: _____

Science: _____

Social studies: _____

Health: _____

Other: _____

Review: _____

Additional information: _____

*Please list specific topics and vocabulary you would like me to pre-teach or review.
**Please attach needed material.

---

at the middle school level. On each sheet, she requests information in the area of academic vocabulary and on specific topics needing to be pre-taught. That way, when ESL teachers begin to co-teach with content-area specialists, they can maximize precious planning time. A sample of how a co-teacher filled out this form follows. Textbox 4.10 is a co-teaching lesson-planning form that integrates all the information discussed in this chapter.

TEXTBOX 4.9.
Sample Collaborative Planning Sheet

Gatelot Elementary ESL   Mrs. Aristea Lucas

ESL Content-Area Support Form

Student: _____

For the week of: _____

Teacher: Mrs. Kelly Benson

Spelling: Lesson #20, We are working on words that end in *le* and *en*.

Math: Lessons #84–88. This week we will be concentrating on multiplying by 10s, 100s, and 1,000s. We will also be starting two-digit x two-digit multiplication.

Science: _____

Social Studies: We are continuing to work on the American Revolution. Student x is gathering facts about his topic, which is "The Battle of Lexington and Concord." He will put his facts into a cohesive paragraph.

Health: _____

Other: _____

Review: The American Revolution test will be next week. Please review the causes of the Revolution with him. You can also review key vocabulary: *Parliament, taxation without representation, militia, redcoats, The Stamp Act, The Sugar Act,* and the *Boston Tea Party*.

Additional Information: Feel free to use the attached worksheets as you see fit.

> **TEXTBOX 4.10.**
> **A Co-teaching Lesson-Planning Form**
>
> **Lesson title:**
>
> **Co-teachers:**
>
> **Subject:**
>
> **Date:**
>
> **Academic content:**
>
>   Vocabulary:
>
>   Content-specific vocabulary (tier 1, tier 2, tier 3):
>
>   Grammar:
>
>   Language structures:
>
> **Co-teaching objectives:**
>
> **Presentation:**
>
>   Type of model:
>
>   Focus on form/fluency (if relevant):
>
>   Who will do what?
>
>   What will ELL students do?
>
> **Practice**
>
>   Type of model
>
>   Focus on form/fluency (if relevant)
>
>   Who will do what?
>
>   What will ELL students do?
>
> **Pre:**
>
>   What will co-teachers do to support content knowledge and vocabulary?
>
>   What will co-teachers need to scaffold?

> **During:**
>
> **Post:**
>
> **Follow-up**
>
> Type of model:
>
> Focus on form/fluency (if relevant):
>
> Who will do what?
>
> What will ELL students do?
>
> Notes:
>
> *Possible co-teaching objectives*: To clarify new academic concepts, to ask and answer questions, to make note of new vocabulary in context and to encourage ELL students to use it in their partner exchange.
>
> *Link to fluency and accuracy*: Co-teachers may need to emphasize accuracy and fluency depending on how much guided practice they have taught. For example, when setting up a partner reading, they can spend some time modeling large, meaningful phrases, as revealed below.
>
> - Encourage ELL students to use large, meaningful phrases.
> - Encourage ELL students to avoid word-by-word slow-downs.
> - Encourage ELL students to use expressive interpretation guided by punctuation and meaning.

PUTTING DIFFERENTIATION AND COLLABORATION INTO CO-TEACHING ACTION

When differentiating academic content in a collaborative context, each student works at a level of challenge appropriate to his readiness needs. In a differentiated classroom, co-teachers tier assignments, projects, learning centers, homework, and even assessments. The concept of tiering is an instructional approach by which all students work with the same key learning goals but at different "degrees of difficulty." As a way of thinking about differentiated teaching for ELL students, "each student needs and deserves a teacher who will be an active partner in helping that student identify and build upon personal strengths and identify and address areas of weakness" (Tomlinson, 2006).

In determining which model is most effective, teachers need to ask which model is most effective for their differentiated teaching goals. For example, which model will give students the most opportunities to progress in the language and content domains of English language learning? The self-assessment below reviews three of the most commonly used co-teaching models that can be used to initially decide which co-teaching model works best with differentiation.

Self-assessment: Of the Three Co-teaching Models, Which Would Be Most Suitable for Delivering a Differentiated Context of Instruction?

1. Both teachers direct the class and are in front of the class:
   a. The core teacher teaches content.
   b. The ESL teacher provides examples, clarifies, uses visuals, restates, etc.
2. Switching roles 50 percent of class time:
   a. The core teacher teaches.
   b. The ESL teacher monitors or assesses students.
   c. Then they switch roles.
3. Class is divided in half and both teach the same content to a heterogeneous group. Both teachers are well skilled in sheltering content (teaching vocabulary, reading comprehension skills, and writing for a specific content area).

A Step-by-Step Process for Planning Differentiation

1. Gather enough information using pre-assessments of students' oral, reading, writing, and speaking backgrounds.
2. Decide on a co-teaching format that best engages and challenges ELL students academically.
3. Decide on a co-teaching format that best suits academic instructional goals. Questions to ask: How will this model help ELL students progress in four language domains? How will this model help ELL students progress through the different proficiency levels?
4. Decide on a co-teaching delivery of instruction that provides oral language instruction and practice while emphasizing content, reading, and writing.

Teachers will want to discuss how their roles can be used to differentiate vocabulary and reading instruction. When co-teachers discuss possible configurations to support differentiation, they may need to spend time discussing

Table 4.2. Same Activity, Different Tasks

Skill	Lower-Performing Group	Middle Group	Stronger Group
Listening	Students list names of people, places, numbers.	Students list names of people, places, numbers, and what they refer to.	Students make up their own questions.
Writing	List—brainstorm words that are relevant to the topic. Use of graphs and pictures.	Students list sentences that are relevant to the topic. Guided composition.	Free essay/composition
Reading	Students extract and list all names of people, places, and numbers and classify them into groups. Students work only with a specific paragraph, looking for specific information. Have students underline all the words they know. Ask them to look up the difficult words. These students become the experts. T/F-type questions.	Students answer questions that relate to general ideas. Multiple-choice-type questions T/F questions but students correct the false questions and/or give evidence from the text.	Oral reports on a text Questions for reading between the lines Answer detailed questions on the text. Make up questions and swap with partner.

students' oral, reading, and vocabulary backgrounds. The rationale of table 4.2 demonstrates how teachers can modify lessons without creating a separate lesson for ELL students. In this chart, teachers adapt a reading task to two or three different levels, thereby enabling the student to choose the level she can most likely function with. The idea is that the teacher learns to adapt already-existing activities without having to make up additional exercises. Teachers can use these ideas to differentiate content across subject areas.

Best Practices in the Classroom: Differentiated Teaching Techniques

At Richland School District One in South Carolina, Stella Kebamke, a third-through fifth-grade teacher, collaborated with a social studies teacher to support content-area vocabulary instruction using a push-in model. Using a variety of prepared games and activities, the content-area teacher pre-taught and reinforced general and content-area vocabulary. Stella Kebamke used easier texts, read to the students, or had them listen to the content on tape. She often summarized the information and presented it to them orally. She used background-knowledge techniques and sometimes used their native language (Spanish) while the social studies teacher taught the core material, concepts, and areas of instruction. When the time came for students to read the text, they had a solid background and understanding of concepts.

In addition, she orally narrated almost all the concepts in the form of oral history. Together, they created characters, scenes, costumes, and dramatized conflicts and revolutions, colonists, and treaties. They tried to personalize abstract content as much as possible using role-play and oral narration. They both read the textbook and retold the story orally. Prior to reading the text, they had a solid background and understanding of concepts. Students felt confident, for example, explaining concepts like *boycott* in their own words. They were able to comprehend and personalize information better. By using these techniques consistently, her ELL students increased their performance on state standard tests at the end of the year.

CHAPTER SUMMARY

ESL and general-education teachers benefit greatly from collaborating on academic language and texts across content areas as well as integrating a balanced literacy program that emphasizes read-alouds and differentiating reading instruction along with other skills. The critical need to successfully collaborate for the sake of ELL students from early to middle elementary grades makes collaboration not only beneficial but also necessary.

There are many models and configurations of collaboration among ESL and general-education teachers that yield effective instruction to meet the diverse academic and language-development needs of ELL students, as described in this chapter. The ultimate goal is to create a supportive learning environment for teachers and students.

STUDY GROUP DISCUSSION QUESTIONS

Use the following link to access a number of videos of teachers sharing their experiences with collaboration: www.cehd.umn.edu/CI/faculty/projects/bigelow/collab.html.

- Discuss the model and its strengths and connection to ESL models.
- What specifically is needed to bridge early and middle primary reading instruction and proficiency levels? How does collaboration enter the picture?

SUGGESTED ACTIVITIES FOR FURTHER COLLABORATION

Summarize the key messages from chapters 3 and 4. Discuss the implications for your school and the ELL population that your school serves. Plan the changes you will make.

Discuss the implications of background knowledge for the academic achievement of ELL students in your school. What is needed to close these gaps? Is it cultural knowledge? Content knowledge? A combination of these? Something else? Find a teacher who has found a way to elicit students' background knowledge around similar content, themes, or vocabulary you are currently teaching. Try this particular strategy or adapt it using another. Discuss your findings. What works? What didn't? What's next?

WEB SOURCES

"Glossary for Teachers and Suggested Lists of Mathematical Language by Grade Level": www.p12.nysed.gov/ciai/mst/math/glossary

"Challenges for ELL students in Content Area Learning": www.everythingesl.net/inservices/challenges_ells_content_area_l_65322.php

"Preparing an Engaging Social Studies Lesson for English Language Learners," by Kristina Robertson and Colorín Colorado (2010): www.ldonline.org/article/35950

"ELLs and Social Studies" (includes examples of language difficulties, text analysis, and strategies for teaching content and language): http://steinhardt.nyu.edu/scms-Admin/uploads/004/740/NYU_PTE_SocialStudies_for_ELLS_Oct2009.pdf

REFERENCES

August, D., & Shanahan, T. (Eds.) (2006). Executive summary. *Developing literacy in second-language learners: Report of the National Literacy Panel on Language-Minority Children and Youth*. Mahwah, NJ: Lawrence Erlbaum Associates. Retrieved January 8, 2009, from www.cal.org/projects/archive/nlpreports/Executive_Summary.pdf

Beck, I. L., & McKeown, M. G. (2001). Text talk: Capturing the benefits of read-aloud experiences for young children. *The Reading Teacher, 55*, 10–20.

Calderon, M. E. (2011a) *Teaching reading and comprehension to English learners, K–5*. Bloomington, IN: Solution Tree.

Calderon, M. (2011b). *Teaching reading to English language learners in K–5th grades*. Bloomington, IN: The Solution Tree Press.

Chall, J., & Dale, E. (1995). *Readability revisited*. Cambridge, MA: Brookline.

Cunningham, A. E., & Stanovich, K. E. (1991). Tracking the unique effects of print exposure in children: Associations with vocabulary, general knowledge and spelling. *Journal of Educational Psychology, 83,* 264–274.

Denton, C. A., & Hocker, J. L. (2006). *Responsive reading instruction: Flexible intervention for struggling readers in the early grades*. Longmont, CO: Sopris West.

Fisher, D., Flood, J., Lapp, D., & Frey, N. (2004). Interactive read-alouds: Is there a common set of implementation practices. *The Reading Teacher, 58,* 8–17.

Friend, M., & Cook, L. (2004). Collaborating with professionals and parents without being overwhelmed: Building partnerships and teams. In J. Burnett & C. Peters-Johnson (Eds.), *Thriving as a special educator* (pp. 29–39). Arlington, VA: The Council for Exceptional Children.

Haager, D., & Windmueller, M. P. (2001). Early reading intervention for English language learners at-risk for learning disabilities: Student and teacher outcomes in an urban school. *Learning Disability Quarterly, 24,* 235–250.

Livingstone, C., et al. (Eds.) (1987). *The Longman guide to graded reading*. Harlow, England: Longman.

Roskos, K. A., Tabors, P. O., & Lenhart, L. A. (2004). *Oral language and early literacy in preschool*. Newark, DE: International Reading Association.

Sasson, D. (2007). Building fluency for struggling ELLs. Retrieved June 27, 2013, from http://ezinearticles.com/?Building-Fluency-For-Struggling-ELLs&id=4172176

Tomlinson, C. A., & Cooper, J. M. (2006). *An educator's guide to differentiating instruction*. Boston: Houghton Mifflin.

Wilson, K. (2003). *Bear Snores On*. New York: Simon and Schuster.

Appendix

**OUTLINE OF ISSUES TO BE DECIDED BETWEEN
GENERAL EDUCATION TEACHERS AND ESL TEACHERS**

Who does what? Issues to be decided between general education teachers and ESL teachers prior to teaching an integrated content lesson

At the onset of collaboration, teachers can refer to the following chart to help them plan and allocate specific responsibilities and tasks.

Division of Tasks	ESL Teacher	General Education Teacher	Both
Grouping students according to critical areas of reading instruction.			
Partnering ELL students strategically based on their English proficiency and native languages			
Assessing knowledge base in order to scaffold academic language			
Assessing background information on student's language (similarities/ differences)			
Identifying and classifying words according to tiers			
Evaluation			
Classroom management			
Division of labor			
Parental contact			
Contact with homeroom and other teachers			
Record keeping			

Bear Snores On

For the Teacher – How to Use This Worksheet

Skills: word recognition, active listening
Material: A copy of the read-aloud book, *Bear Snores On*, by Karma Wilson
Procedure: This pre-reading activity prepares students for reading authentic literature. Have students pay close attention to illustrations such as the cover, inside covers and back covers. Write any interesting information on the board. Then have students go through the list of words in Part 1 and circle those words that describe the front cover. As a last step, have students check their answers as you read the correct words aloud.

Before asking students to answer question #2, you may want to preteach the word "snore" by checking students' familiarity with the context. You can start by asking: What does the bear do when he is sleeping?

Name: _____   Grades 1-2

Let's Read: Bear Snores On
Part 1

Directions:

Look at the cover of **Bear Snores On**.
Circle all the words that you see.

bear	dog	raven	mouse	bus
hare	leaves	school	cat	badger

Now, listen to your teacher read the words to you.
How many words did you get right?_____

Now look at the title: **Bear Snores On**.

Is bear sleeping or is he awake? Write your answer here:
_____

For the Teacher – How to Use this Worksheet

Skill: The worksheet promotes word recognition and writing
Procedure: This pre-reading activity prepares students for the reading activity in part 3. Say and write the title of the book on the board. This is an opportunity to emphasize individual letters or blends. Students look, say and write the author's name. As a last step, say the illustrator's name and point out that the illustrator and author may be the same person. Have students look, say and write the illustrator's name.

For question #2, encourage students to predict what they think the story will be about using WH guiding questions. Encourage them to use the words from part 1. Encourage one or two word responses depending on students' oral abilities. A brainstorm technique can be ideal especially when working with heterogeneous classes. Now your students are ready to confirm their predictions.

Name: _____   Grades 1-2

Let's Read: Bear Snores On
Part 2

Directions:

Look at the title.
Say the title.
Write the title of the book:_____

Look at the name of the author.
Say the name of the author.
Write the name of the author: _____

Look at the name of the illustrator.
Say the name of the illustrator.
Write the name of the illustrator: _____

Tell your partner what you think the story is about. Use the words from part 1. Use these question words to help you: **Who? What? When? How? How much? Where? Why?**

Now, listen to your teacher read you the story.

For the Teacher – How to Use this Worksheet

Skills: active listening, reading comprehension, understanding vocabulary in context
Procedure: After stopping at various places in the read-aloud to confirm predictions, have students recall the beginning of the story. Model for students by rereading specific parts of the read-aloud for students as necessary. You might want to help students understand that the word "tunnel" can be both a verb and a noun by asking this question: **When you tunnel up through the floor, are you on top of the ground or underneath?**

Name: _____   Grades 1-2

Let's Read: Bear Snores On
Part 3

Directions:

1. Circle the correct answer.

At **the beginning** of the story, what is bear doing?

a. He is reading a book.

b. He is snoring.

c. He is eating popcorn.

2. Read this sentence from the story and answer the questions.

A gopher and a mole tunnel up through the floor. Then a wren and a raven flutter in through the door!

Which animals dug a tunnel?_____ _____
Which animals come in through the door?
_____ _____

For the Teacher – How to Use this Worksheet

Skills: word recognition, reading comprehension, understanding vocabulary in context
Procedure: This activity addresses the relationship between **cause and effect**. You might want to first address the concept of **cause** by saying: "something happens in our story to *cause* bear to finally stop his snoring. Do you remember what it is? Let's read it again together and see if we can find the word (or words) that tell(s) us what causes bear to suddenly wake up."Then read the passage together and confirm responses. Discuss the term **effect**. What **effect** does bear's sneeze have on all the animals? Ask: What **effect** do the animals' reactions have in the story? If bear's sneeze **causes** the animals to hide from the noise or run away, what is the **effect**, *or what happens*, because of those actions? Use the pictures as a lead-in. Have students find another word for "standing still." Have students complete the passage about bear using the verbs from the story. As a final step, see what students can infer about bear based on his descriptive actions.

Name: _____   Grades 1-2
Let's Read: Bear Snores On
Part 4

Directions:
Read this paragraph from the story.
Hare stokes the fire.
Mouse seasons stew.
Then a small pepper fleck
Makes the bear…RAAAAA-CHOOOOOO!

How does bear finally wake up?
Circle the correct answer:
a. Bear hears a noise.
b. Bear smells some pepper.
c. Mouse and hare wake up the bear.
d. Bear becomes hungry.

After bear sneezes, what do all the animals do?
  a. They sneeze.
  b. They laugh.
  c. They eat stew.
  d. They stand still.

Can you find another word in the story for "standing still"?
Write the word here: _____

What happens after the animals freeze? Complete the passage using the words from the story.
Bear _____ and he _____.
Bear _____ and he _____!
Bear _____ and he _____.
Bear _____ and he _____!
What does this tell you about bear? _____

Appendix

For the Teacher – How to Use This Worksheet
Skills: reading comprehension, word recognition
Procedure: Have students reread part(s) of the story and answer the questions.

Name: _____   Grades 1-2

Let's Read: Bear Snores On
Part 5

Directions:

Now reread the story and see if you can answer these questions:

1. At the **beginning** of the story, **where** does bear snore?
a. in your house
b. in a cave
c. in a supermarket

2. **Who** comes into the cave while bear is snoring?

Circle all the names of the correct animals:

cat	mouse	dog	zebra	hare
horse	badger	snake	mole	frog
gopher	lion	wren	tiger	cheetah

3. **What** happens when the sun comes up?

Circle the correct answer.

    a. Bear and his friends snore.
    b. Bear's friends snore but bear can't sleep.
    c. Bear and his friends tell stories.

For the Teacher – How to Use This Worksheet

Skills: word recognition, active listening, sound correspondences

Procedure: Point out the rhyme scheme of the story. Ask which two words rhyme using the sentences "Mouse sips wee slurps. Hare burps big BURPS!" Continue by looking at the rhyme scheme for mouse and hare and ask: Which word describes what the hare does? Which word describes what mouse does?

Name: _____   Grades 1-2

Let's Read: Bear Snores On
Part 6

Directions:

Read the sentence: Mouse sips wee slurps. Hare burps big BURPS!

Which two words rhyme?
Write them here: _____   _____

Now read these:

1.
In a cave in the woods,
in his deep, dark lair,
through the long, cold winter
sleeps a great brown bear.

Which two words rhyme?
Write them here: _____   _____

2.
And the bear wakes up! Bear gnarls and he snarls.
Bear roars and he rumbles! Bear jumps and he stomps.
Bear growls and he grumbles.

Which words rhyme?
Write the rhyming pairs here: _____   _____
_____   _____

Appendix

For the Teacher – How to Use this Worksheet

Skills: This worksheet promotes word recognition, verbal questioning, talking with a partner and sentence completion.
Procedure: Pair each student with a partner. Have students talk to their partner to get the information to fill in the worksheet. Next, have the students go back to the initial word list from part 1 to see how many words they now recognize. Discuss any improvements they've made in recognizing the words on the list.

Name: _____   Grades 1-2

Let's Read: Bear Snores On
Part 7

Directions:

Talk to your partner and fill in the blanks.

My partner's favorite character in the story is _____
because_____.

My partner's least favorite character in the story is_____
because _____.

My partner's favorite story is _____.

My partner's least favorite story is _____.

Directions:

Now, read these words –

bear	cave	hare	wren
snore	mouse	winter	woods
badger	mole		

Listen to your teacher read the words to you.
How many words did you know this time? _____

Index

academic language: comprehension problems, 23, 59; listening skills and, 23, 24; objectives for, 34, *35*; tiers, 27, *35,* 78–79. *See also* vocabulary
academic talk, 25, 28
addition lesson, email follow-up on, 77–78
administrative support, xx; and curriculum constraints, 7; methods of, 14–15; for professional development, 14; and time constraints, 5–6
affective domains, in reading, 52–53
Allington, R. L. A., 17

background knowledge, 52–57; assessments, 52–53; definition of, 53; instructional planning around, 54; strategies for building, 54–57, 88
balanced literacy approach, 60; push-in model for, example of, 76–77
Barkon, Elisheva, 63
Barone, Diane, ix, 54
Bear Snores On (Wilson), 63, 66, 74
Broersma, M., 24
Brown, Clara Lee, 10, 18, 49

Calderon, M. E., 9–10, 14, 27, 49, 68, 69, 75, 78–79

California, xiv
cause and effect, scenario for teaching, 66
characters, working with, 65
class division, 10, 48
classroom constraints: curriculum-related, 7; time-related, 5–6
cognitive domains, in reading, 52–53
collaboration: history of, 2–3; increase in, xiv; integration of skills taught in, xix–xx; lack of, consequences of, 7–8; need for, xiii–xiv, 3, 4–5; obstacles to, 1, 5–7; present-day, 3; and seeing the "bigger picture," xv; in special education, 2–3, 18–19; steps in, 36–37; at whole-school level, 14. *See also* co-teaching
collaborative models, 10–14; for building background knowledge, 54–55; class division, 10, 46; co-planning, example of, 43–45; definition of, 8; for differentiated instruction, 86; for ELLs, 8–9; group, 13; inclusion, 17–18; for learning-disabled ELLs, 18–19; parallel teaching, 13; pull-out, 12; push-in, 12, 76–77, 87–88; for reading instruction for young ELLs (K-2), 47–48; switching roles, 10, 11, 46,

101

68; turn-taking, 10, 46, 54. *See also* team teaching
collaborative planning. *See* co-planning
collocations, 26–27
Common Core State Standards (CCSS), xiv, 4, 47
comprehensible input/content, 29–31; strategies for, *30*
comprehension: importance of, 23, 29, 59; listening as support for, xix, 28, 29–31, *30*. *See also* reading comprehension
content-area instruction: balanced literacy approach to, example, 76–77; and CCSS, xiv; co-planning support sheet, 79, 82, *82, 83*; differentiated, 79, 85–88; ELL-based resource platform for, 4; integrated approach to, xix; oral goals and methods, *64–65*; for reading fluency, *81*; reading materials, 56
content-area vocabulary. *See* academic language
content learning log, 55
content schemata, 52
context, in vocabulary instruction, 50–52, 63, 74
Cook, L., 60
co-planning: content-area support sheet, 79, 82, *82, 83*; email for, 77–78; for reading instruction, 43–45
co-teaching: email follow-up, 77–78; framework, 9–13; lesson-planning form, 82, *84–85*; methods, 10–11; requirements, 10
co-teaching models. *See* collaborative models
cultural information, sharing, 55
Curran, M. E., 16
curriculum constraints, 7
Cutler, A., 24

demographic changes, 4
dictation, 25–26

differentiated instruction, 17–18, 85–88; co-teaching model for, 86; example of, 87–88; planning, 86–87; of reading, practices for, 79, *80*; of vocabulary, 78, 79
"direct consulting," 10, 18
direct instruction. *See* team teaching
diversity standards, 15–16
Dove, M., 6

educational standards, 47; TESOL, xxii, 44, 47
Education Week blog, 4
effect, teaching about, 66
Ellis, Rod, 19
email, 77–78
English language learners (ELLs): challenges for, ix–x, 23; general-education teachers of, ix, xiii; grouping by language performance level, 79, 85; increase in, 4; in K–12, 15; with learning disabilities, 16–19; low achievement in, xiii, 7–8; need of support, ix–x, xiv; stakeholders in, 7; term, xxii. *See also* young ELLs (K–2)
English language proficiency, 42–43; assessment, 43; failure to reach standards for, 7–8; grouping ELLs by, 79, 85; in reading, assessment checklist, 43, *44*
error analysis, 19
ESL (English as a second language) (term), xxiii
ESL co-teaching framework, 9–13; as "direct consulting," 10, 18; steps in, 36–37
ESL instruction, oral goals and methods of, *64–65*
ESL teacher: collaboration with general-education teacher, 9–13, 36–37; as SLA expert, 43, 49–50. *See also specific instructional areas, e.g. listening instruction*

ESL team teaching, 18–19. *See also* team teaching

Fernandez, Nicole, 12, 76–78
first grade, collaboration in, 48
fluency: oral, activities for, *64–65*; reading, strategies for building, *81*
form: in pre-teaching vocabulary, 62; questions of, 31; in SLA, 29–31
Friend, M., 60
funding, 5, 7

general-education classroom, oral instructional goals and methods in, *64–65*
general-education teacher: and collaboration, xiii–xiv, xx; collaboration in special education, 2–3, 10, 18–19; collaboration with ESL teacher, 9–13, 36–37; in inclusion model, 18; as teachers of ELLs, ix, xiii. *See also specific instructional areas, e.g.* listening instruction
geology, listening lesson on, 28
Getting to Know Each Other (assessment exercise), 33–34
The Grouchy Ladybug (Carle), 74
group models, 13
Grucelski, Kelly, 28, 43, 45, 47–48
guest speakers, 55
guided reading, *36*

Haager, D., 62
Hakuta, Kenji, 4
Heskett, Tracie, 2, 9, 23
history instruction: example of, 87–88; reading materials for, 56
Honigsfeld, A., 6
Hornbrook and Inkwells (Kay), 56

inclusion model, 17–18
Individualized Education Program (IEP), 2, 3

Individuals with Disabilities Education Act (1997), 2
input hypothesis, 29–31

K-12 education, ELLs as issue in, 15
Kay, Verla, 56
Kebamke, Stella, 87–88
Krashen, Stephen, 29

language-acquisition theory. *See* second-language acquisition
language scaffolds, examples, 74
large group/small group model, 13
Leana, Carrie R., 6
learning disabilities, ELLs with, 16–19
Lenhart, L. A., 62
lesson organizer, *72–73*
lesson-planning form, for co-teaching, 82, *84–85*
linguistic schemata, 52
listening instruction, 23–37; collocations, 26–27; and comprehensible input, 29–31; for comprehension, xix, 28, 29–31, *30*; dictation, 25–26; in isolation, xix; on meaning of text vocabulary, 28; for pronunciation, 25, 26–27; strategies, *30, 31*, 33–34, *36*, 39; throughout reading process, *36*; and vocabulary development, 25
listening skills: and academic language, 23, 24; goals for, identifying, 32, 34, *35*; needs analysis/ assessment, 32, *32*, 33–34; problems in acquiring, 24; and reading comprehension, 24
look-read-say, 62–63
Lucas, Aristea, 79, 82

Malka, Tara, 10
manage (word), 75
map lesson, example, 76–77
Marzano, Robert, 53

math instruction: email follow-up in, 77–78; language objectives for, 47–48
meaning: questions of, 31; in SLA, 29–31. *See also* comprehension
Mondria, J.-A., 50, 51–52
Morrow, L. M., ix

Nation, P., 26–27
National Association for Bilingual Education (NABE), 15, 47
National Council on Accreditation of Teacher Education (NCATE), 15, 16, 47
National Research Council science standards, 4
needs analysis/assessment: for content-area vocabulary, 34, *35*; for listening skills, 32, *32,* 33–34
No Child Left Behind Act (2001), 3

oral fluency, activities for, *64–65*
oral instruction: goals and methods of, *64–65. See also* listening instruction
oral narration, 88
Ozckus, Lori D., 29

parallel teaching, 13
Partnership Academy, 28, 43, 45, 47–48
plot review, 65
predictions, eliciting, 65–66
prior knowledge. *See* background knowledge
PRO (Purpose, Reading concept, Orientation), 75–76
professional development, 14
pronunciation, 25, 26–27
Pulaski Elementary School, 56
push-in models, 12; benefits of, 12, 77; example scenarios, 76–77, 87–88
push-out models, 12

read-alouds, 60–74; activities after, 67–69, *69;* activities before, 60–63; activities during, 65–66; cause and effect instruction example, 66; co-teacher's checklist, *70–71;* lesson organizer, *72–73;* partner reading after, 68–69; planning form, 60, *61;* planning template, *73;* plot and character activities, 65; predictions in, 65–66; summary writing after, 67–68; think-alouds after, 67; vocabulary instruction before, 62–63; vocabulary instruction during, 62, 74
reading, guided, *36*
reading attitudes, 52–53; questionnaire, 53
reading comprehension: assessment checklist, 43, *44;* background knowledge and, 52–53; instructional models for young (K-2) ELLs, 46; listening skills and, 24; SLA issues in, 49–50, *51;* for young ELLs (K-2), 24, 28, 46, 74
reading fluency, strategies for, *81*
reading instruction, 43–57; background knowledge and, 52–57, 88; balanced literacy approach to, 60, 76–77; challenges in, 43; content-area support sheet, 79, 82, *82, 83;* co-planning example, 43–45; co-planning sheets, 79, 82, *82, 83;* co-teaching lesson-planning form, 82, *84–85;* crucial components, 47; differentiated, 79, *80,* 86–88, *87;* in first grade, checklist for, 48; for fluency, *81;* integrated approach to, xix; listening and speaking activities in, *36;* look-read-say, 62–63; oral goals and methods, *64–65;* partner reading, 68–69; planning template, *73;* and PRO, 74–76; standard-driven, and SEAT, 47; summary writing, 67–68; think-alouds, 67; visual aids, *36;* vocabulary instruction in, explicit, 74–75; for young ELLs (K-2), 45–46, 48, 74–75 *See also* read-alouds

reading/literacy specialist: collaboration with ESL teacher, 43, 49–50; ELL assessment checklist for, *44*; SLA issues monitoring table for, *51*; in summary writing, 68
reading materials, 56–57
read-look-say, 62–63
resource constraints, 5–7
resource platform, for content-area instruction of ELLs, 4
Richland School District One, 87
rocks, listening lesson on, 28
Rocky Point School district, 76
Roskos, K. A., 62

Sachem Central School District, 79
Sanchez, M., 14
Sasson, Dorit, 2, 23
schemata theory, 52–53
See also background knowledge
school leadership, support from. *See* administrative support
science instruction, 28, 79
SEAT, 47
second-language acquisition (SLA): error analysis for, 19; ESL teacher as expert in, 43, 49–50; input hypothesis and, 29–31; monitoring table, *51*; and reading comprehension, 49–50, *51*; and reading instruction, 49–50, *51*; research *vs.* practice on, 15; silent period in, 19; and vocabulary acquisition, 50–52
sentence frames/starters, 56, 68
Shah, 16
silent period, 19
SLA. *See* second-language acquisition
Slavin, R. E., 14
"social capital" of teachers, investment in, 6
special education: collaboration in, 2–3, 10, 18–19; for ELLs, 16–19; inclusion model, 17–18
special-education teacher, 10

stakeholders, 7
standards, 47; TESOL, xxii, 47
Standards for Reading Professionals, 15
summary writing, 67–68
switching roles, 10, 11; scenarios for, 46, 68

Tabors, P. O., 62
teacher teams, ESL teacher-led, 18–19
team teaching, 10, 11–12; of ELLs with learning disabilities, 18–19; in partner reading, 68; of young ELLs (K-2), in reading, 45–46
TESOL standards, xxii, 47
think-alouds, 67
tiers/tiering, 85; vocabulary, 27, 34, *35,* 78–79
time constraints, 5–6
Tomlinson, C. A., 67, 85
turn-taking, 10; scenarios for, 46, 54

Ur, Penny, 50

visual aids: for building background knowledge, 55, 56–57; in reading instruction, 36
vocabulary: academic (content-specific), 23, 34, *35,* 59; and academic success, 25, 74; comprehension of, 23, 29; SLA issues in acquiring, 50–52; tiers, 27, 34, *35,* 78–79
vocabulary instruction: background knowledge and, 52–57; collocations, 26–27; comprehensible input in, 29–31; comprehension strategies, *30*; content-area support sheet, 79, 82, *82, 83*; context in, 50–52, 63, 74; co-teaching lesson-planning form, 82, *84–85*; differentiated, 78, 79, 86–88; explicit, 74–75; form, meaning, and accuracy in, 62; listening as support for comprehension in, xix, 28, 29, *30*; look-read-say technique, 62–63; objectives, 32, 34, *35*; oral goals and

methods, *64–65*; and PRO, 75–76; pronunciation, 25, 26–27; before read-alouds, 62–63; during read-alouds, 62, 74; for reading fluency, *81*; in reading instruction, 74–75; SLA issues in, 50–52, *51*; tiering in, 27, 34, *35,* 78–79; word analysis, 45–46; for young ELLs (K-2), 46, 74–75

Windmueller, M. P., 62
word analysis, 45–46
writing instruction: differentiated, *87*; summarizing, 67–68

Xu, S., ix

young ELLs (K-2): English proficiency *vs.* English language proficiency in, 42–43; in first grade, collaboration for, 48; knowledge needed to support, 8; listening and, 24, 28; listening needs analysis/assessment for, 33; reading comprehension development in, 24, 28, 46, 74; reading instruction for, 45–46, 74–75; vocabulary instruction for, 46, 74–75; word analysis scenarios, 45–46

www.ingramcontent.com/pod-product-compliance
Lightning Source LLC
Chambersburg PA
CBHW052132300426
44116CB00010B/1868